ROCK 'N' ROLL

Designer Marianne Llewellyn

Dedicated to Eve and Saffron

Published by Socion Books, Editorial Director Anthony D'Abreu.
Socion Books is an imprint of Sociopack Publications Limited,
2 Crawford Place, London W1H 1JD.

ISBN:

INTRODUCTION

Rock and Roll was at the peak of its commercial and musical success from 1955 to 1960, and this book concentrates on that period: its pre-history has been well documented elsewhere, and immediate developments like High School have not been included because they really require a book to themselves.

Surprisingly little has been written about the actual lives of fifties rock and rollers, apart from a handful of the major stars. So the first half of this book contains biographies of some forty rock and rollers who emerged during the mid-fifties. Following each biography is a discography. These are intended to be of practical use to record collectors, and are complemented by a chapter on present-day sources for buying fifties' releases.

Most first-generation British rock and roll was pretty dire, or pretty funny, depending on your point of view. But some of it was good, and the better manifestations are covered here. The most successful local rock and rollers are included in the biographies/discographies section and another chapter looks at 'Oh Boy', a TV series which to date has only been rivalled for authenticity and excitement by 'Ready Steady Go' in Britain and 'Soul Train' in the States.

Together with the remaining chapters, in particular the one about rock and roll movies, a comprehensive account of the music and its performers is built up. But no overall critique has been attempted. You are your own critic, this book is a celebration.

HANK BALLARD

Hank Ballard is probably best remembered as the man who wrote and first recorded 'The Twist', the dance-craze song which launched Chubby Checker into a hit-making career in 1960, and spawned a fad which dominated pop music for a while during 1962. However his career as a writer/performer in the R&B world goes back a good deal further.

At the beginning of the 1950's, he was lead vocalist with a group called the Royals, who recorded for Federal, a subsidiary of the King label in Cincinnatti. They scored several successes in the strictly black R&B market of the time, mostly with close-harmony ballad stylings, like 'Every Beat of My Heart' which was their biggest hit in 1953. Then in 1954 they made a disc in complete contrast to their normal material, 'Work With Me Annie', an uptempo number with the accent not on the vocals or the melody, but on the rhythm and the lyrics, which were delivered in unambiguous style by Ballard and were most blatantly sexual, 'Work With Me Annie, Let's Get While Gitting is Good, Annie Please Don't Cheat, Give Me All My Meat'.

As soon as the record showed signs of big success, the group decided to sever connections with their old style and sell themselves as a new outfit: the name on the label of 'Work With Me Annie' quickly changed from the Royals to the Midnighters. The disc became number one in the R&B market, at the time quite distinct and separate from the pop charts, and sold upwards of a million copies. It was then followed by a whole series of very similar songs, mostly written by Ballard himself, whose lyrics continued 'Annie's' bumpy saga. 'Sexy Ways' was another R&B number one, as was 'Annie Had a Baby', while 'Annie's Aunt Fannie' and 'Ashamed of Myself' enjoyed healthy sales.

Ballard became a sort of folk hero for the black record buyers, who looked forward to a good belly laugh with each succeeding release. The pop market, however, was completely unaware of him, since suggestive lyrics were taboo on white radio stations, and if an R&B song was considered 'suitable', it was normally covered by a white artist anyway. Effectively, this meant that Hank and the Midnighters were by-passed during the early rise of Rock'n'Roll, because all their best material had gone unheard before the music became 'de-segregised' on the radio, and none of their discs of the years 1955-58 proved distinctive enough to draw attention to the group amidst the welter of newly-successful R&B talent.

It was not until early in 1959, when many of the groups who had been their contemporaries had broken up or disappeared into obscurity, that 'Teardrops On Your Letter' at last provided a national Top 100 hit for the group, who had now expanded their billing to 'Hank Ballard and The Midnighters'. The disc only reached No. 93, but on the flipside was the Ballard-penned tune which was later to reap such handsome reward, 'The Twist'.

A cover version of Wilbert Harrison's 'Kansas City' gave Hank a second minor hit, and then he failed to click again for three or four releases before coming up with his biggest-ever smash, 'Finger Poppin' Time'. This made the charts in May 1960, and stayed in for exactly six months, climbing to number 7 and earning a gold disc. Suddenly, the Midnighters were the R&B dance record kings. 'Let's Go, Let's Go, Let's Go' sold almost as well as its predecessor, reaching number 6 in a healthy four month chart stay, while also into the U.S. Top 30 went 'The Hoochie Coochie Coo' and 'The Twist'. The latter was reactivated primarily because of the new cover version by Chubby Checker, and while it couldn't match Checker's rapid climb to number one and consequent million-plus sale, the Ballard version held its own in the Top 100 for 16 weeks, creaming off a healthy proportion of the sales.

1961 continued Hank's consistent run of hits, and he made very little attempt to get away from the beaty novelty dance style which 'Finger Poppin'' had started. 'Let's Go Again', 'The Continental Walk', 'The Switch-a-Roo', 'The Float', 'Nothin' But Good' and 'Keep On Dancing' all chased each other into the charts in quick succession. Then, at the very beginning of 1962, Chubby Checker's 'Twist' suddenly became a number one hit all over again. The Twist became a world-wide dance craze and a pop phenomenon, and suddenly everybody was cutting dance discs and Twist hits. Hank was almost literally lost in the rush. He had a brief touch with a cash-in of his own, 'Do You Know How to Twist?' in February of 1962, but the disc only rose to number 82, and he didn't see the

Hank Ballard date unknown

charts again.

For almost a decade, Hank and the Midnighters went back to playing and recording in virtual obscurity; singles and albums appeared occasionally on the King label, but none sold very well. During the late sixties the Midnighters broke up. In 1971, Hank came under the wing of James Brown, who produced some new recordings with him and added him to his own team of performers. On a recent James Brown album, Hank can be heard in monologue, rapping about music and telling how Brown salvaged him the 'graveyard of losers'. He may yet have more to offer.

BRITISH RELEASES TO 1960

Singles

1959	'Kansas City', 'The Twist' Parlophone 45R4558
1960	'Finger Poppin' Time', 'I Love You I Love You So' Parlophone 45R 44682
1960	'Teardrops On Your Letter', 'The Twist' Parlophone 45R688

CHUCK BERRY

From 1955 to 1958 Chuck Berry provided rock and roll with getting on for thirty of its best ever songs. Timeless classics which have as much impact today as they did when he first wrote them: 'Maybelline', 'Wee Wee Hours', 'Thirty Days', 'Roll Over Beethoven', 'Too Much Monkey Business', 'Brown Eyed Handsome Man', 'School Days', 'Rock and Roll Music', 'Sweet Little Sixteen', 'Reelin' and Rocking', 'Johnny B. Goode', 'Around and Around', 'Oh Carol', 'Little Queenie', 'Back in The USA', 'Memphis Tennessee', 'Let It Rock', 'Nadine'.

> *She drew out all her money at the Southern Trust,*
> *And put her little boy aboard a Greyhound bus,*
> *Leaving Louisiana for the golden West*
> *Down came the tears from her happiness*
> *Her own little son named Johnny B. Goode*
> *Was gonna make some motion-pictures out in Hollywood.*
>
> *Bye bye bye bye*
> *Bye bye bye bye*
> *Bye bye Johnny*
> *Goodbye Johnny B. Goode.*
>
> *She remembered taking money earnt from gathering crops*
> *And buying Johnny's guitar at a broker's shop.*
> *As long as he could play it by the rail-road side,*
> *And wouldn't get in trouble she was satisfied.*
> *But never thought there'd ever come a day like this*
> *When she would have to give her son a goodbye kiss.*
>
> *Bye bye bye bye*
> *Bye bye bye bye*
> *Bye bye Johnny*
> *Goodbye Johnny B. Goode.*
>
> *She finally got the letter she'd been dreaming of*
> *Johnny wrote and told her he had fell in love,*
> *As soon as he was married he would bring her back,*
> *And build a mansion for them by the railroad track.*
> *So every time they heard the locomotive roar*
> *They'd be standing a-waitin' in the kitchen door.*
>
> *Bye bye bye bye*
> *Bye bye bye bye*
> *Bye bye Johnny*
> *Goodbye Johnny B. Goode.*
>
> Bye bye Johnny (Berry)
> Jewel Music Publishing Company.

His lyrics dealt mainly with cars, girls and rock and roll music, and he was undoubtedly the best lyricist of fifties rock. But just as important was his feel for rhythm. He'd bend it, kick it, throw it up in the air, twiddle it round his fingers, but always, bang, he'd come right back on it like it was a series of rocks he was jumping across. And his stage presence too, the duck walk, the way he moved the guitar around in his hands: he was a real artist, and still is.

He was born Charles Edward Berry in St. Louis, Missouri, about 40 years ago. He attended Sumner High School in St. Louis, where he sang bass in the Glee Club. In his early teens he took guitar, teaching himself from a chord book.

In 1952 he started his own group, the Chuck Berry Combo, working clubs in St. Louis. While on a long contract at the Cosmopolitan Club in the city he flew to Chicago where he visited the clubs and met Muddy Waters, who encouraged him to go and see Leonard and Phil Chess at Chess Records. Shortly afterwards in May 1955 Chuck had his first recording session with the Chess brothers.

At the session were rock and roll DJs/fans Alan Freed and Russ Fratto, and they are credited with part-composition of the song recorded at that session, 'Maybelline'. Their influence is marked in the rather plodding Haley-type rhythm of the piece: Chuck's later songs were rarely so rigid, his rhythmic patterns were strong but flexible.

Anyway, 'Maybelline' was a massive hit, and was awarded the Billboard Triple Award for being the biggest selling R&B record in

Chuck Berry 1955, the first Chess publicity photo

the nation, the most played R&B record on the nation's juke boxes, and the most played R&B record on the nation's radio stations.

From then till 1959 Chuck was at his peak in the States, touring constantly and getting hits constantly. He was the only artist hired in 1956,57 and 58 for each and every Super Attractions 'Big Show of Stars', the biggest of the travelling road shows of the time.

The personnel on most of his fifties records was Willie Dixon, bass, Freddie Bellow, drums, Lafayette Leake, piano, and Johnny Johnson, sax. This band in some conbination or other also backed Chess artists Muddy Waters and Howlin Wolf on many of their recordings.

From 1959 to 1964 Chuck's popularity declined and he didn't have any more big hits in the States. Partly because his musical energies were at a low ebb, temporarily as it turned out, but also because of some bad publicity and a two-year jail term he received for a so-called abduction of an 'under age' girl. However 1963/4 saw a big increase in his popularity in Britain. The new wave of British R&B bands like the Stones started recording many of his fifties tracks, and he himself had top twenty hits with Pye re-issues of 'Memphis Tennessee', 1963, and 'No Particular Place To Go', 1964.

In 1965 Chuck left Chess records, for reasons that are still unclear, and started recording in Memphis for Mercury. He stayed with Mercury till 1970 and that's about all there is to say about the period. He did little strong recording and on live appearances concentrated on simply performing his fifties numbers.

In 1970 he returned to Chess and the first album with the label 'Back Home' was . . . . fantastic. Chuck Berry was back. The new songs were as good as the fifties ones and, refreshingly, had little in common with them stylistically. The band on the album was superb, as opposed to the plodding bands used on the Mercury releases.

Since 'Back Home', Chuck has released two new albums, 'San Francisco Dues' and the 'London Chuck Berry Sessions'. He is still very much around, and if Mrs. Mary Whitehouse carries on listening to his lyrics and his rhythm, who knows what could happen?

BRITISH RELEASES TO 1960
+British Top 20 Hit

Singles

June 56   'Down Bound Train', 'No Money Down' London 45HLU8275

Feb 57   'Havana Moon', 'You Can't Catch Me' London 45HLN8375

June 57   'Driftin' Heart', 'Roll Over Beethoven' London 45HLU8428

Jan 58   'Blue Feeling', 'Rock and Roll Music' London 45HL8531

Apr 58   'Reelin' and Rockin ', 'Sweet Little Sixteen' London 45HLM8585+

June 58   'Around and Around', 'Johnny B. Goode' London 45HLM8629

Sept 58   'Beautiful Delilah', 'Vacation Time' London 45HLM8677

Nov 58   'Carol' 'Hey Pedro' London 45HL8712

Dec 58   'Joe Joe Gun', 'Sweet Little Rock and Roll' London 45HL8767

May 59   'Almost Grown', 'Little Queenie' London 45HLM8853

July 59   'Back in the USA', 'Memphis Tennessee' London 45HLM8921

Mar 60   'Let It Rock', 'Too Pooped To Pop' London 45HLM9069

July 60   'Bye Bye Johnny', 'Mad Lad. London 45HLM9159

EPs

1957   'Maybelline' 'Wee Wee Hours', 'Thirty Days', 'Together' London 1053

1959   'Reelin' and Rockin ', 'Rock and Roll Music', 'Sweet Little Sixteen', 'Guitar Boogie' London 1188

LPs

1958   'One Dozen Berries', 'Sweet Little Sixteen', 'Blue Feeling', 'Lajaunda', 'Rockin' at the Philarmonic', 'Oh Baby Doll', 'Reelin' and Rockin ', 'Ingo' 'Rock and Roll Music', 'How You've Changed', 'Low Feeling', 'It Don't Take But a Few Minutes' London HA-M2132

Chuck Berry, 1956, Chess photo

The Big Bopper 1958

THE BIG BOPPER

The Big Bopper, real name Jape Richardson, was norn on 24th October 1932, in Sabine Pass, Texas. He graduated to being a rock star through an already successful career as a disc jockey, where he used a flamboyant, lecherous, laughing characterisation of the Bopper with great success.

Richardson had started his radio career during his college days in Texas, when a part-time job on the airwaves and several appearances as a singer/comic not only kept the pennies coming in, but also served as a good training ground for his Big Bopper act. He became programme director at Radio KTRM in Beaumont Texas in 1955, the very start of the rock era.

Jape had taken to writing songs in his spare time off the air, and it was naturally not very long before he started looking around for an outlet for this side of his talent. Mercury records signed him as a singer, and Jape cut a couple of discs under his own name; fairly straight country-style efforts. They were completely unsuccessful, and the career of Jape Richardson C&W singer was quickly terminated.

The answer was obvious, and a shrewd Jape Richardson did not miss it. The Big Bopper replaced his real-life name on disc, and a hilarious but highly commercial rock'n'roll style replaced the Country songs. The first disc to be cut was 'Chantilly Lace', backed with an answer song to two other recent novelty rock hits in 'The Purple People Eater Meets the Witch Doctor'. It was an instant smash, and roared into the U.S. Top 100 on August 10th, 1958, where it was to remain for no less than 25 weeks! It climbed to No. 6, and he received a gold disc for a million-plus sales.

The Big Bopper joined the familiar rock star pattern of nationwide TV appearances and multi-venue, multi-star touring caravans. 'Chantilly Lace' became a hit in England, and he had a second U.S. success with the follow-up disc 'Big Bopper's Wedding', 'Little Red Riding Hood', both sides of which made the charts strongly. At the turn of the year Richardson was at his peak, with these singles and an album selling in vast quantities. He joined another all-star tour which included on its bill Buddy Holly, the Crickets and Ritchie Valens, and they began another round-the-country trek. Then came the night in Fargo, North Dakota, February 3rd 1959, when the artists became snowbound. It was a choice between spending an uncomfortable night in Fargo or attempting to charter a plane to take them to another town and a hotel. Holly, Valens and the Big Bopper chose the latter and they died when the plane crashed in a blizzard in the foothills of the North Dakotan mountains.

Though many of his records verged on the mechanical, the quality of 'Chantilly Lace' has kept him a rock and roll favourite to date.

BRITISH RELEASES TO 1960
+British Top 20 Hit
Singles
1958   'Chantilly Lace', 'Purple People Eater Meets The Witch Doctor' Mercury 45AMT 1002
1958   'Big Bopper's Wedding', 'Little Red Riding Hood' Mercury 45AMT1017
1959   'It's What I'm Talking About' Mercury 45AMT1046

EPs
1959   'Chantilly Lace', 'Purple People Eater Meets The Witch Doctor', 'Big Bopper's Wedding', 'Little Red Riding Hood' Mercury 10004

LPs
1959   'Chantilly Lace', 'Pink Petticoats', 'The Clock', 'Walkin' Through My Dreams', 'Someone Watching Over You', 'Old Maid', 'Big Bopper's Wedding', 'Little Red Riding Hood', 'Preacher and the Bear', 'It's The Truth Ruth', 'White Lightning', 'Strange Kisses' Mercury MMC14008

THE COASTERS

The group later to achieve rock'n'roll fame as the Coasters was actually formed in 1950 under a different name, the Robins. The quartet Billy Guy, Carl Gardner, Dub Jones and Bobby Nunn came together in Los Angeles under the direction of an energetic new pair of record producers and songwriters named Jerry Leiber and Mike Stoller. This duo worked on an independent basis, writing for and recording their artists themselves, and then placing the products with one or other of the small R&B labels which existed in California at the time. The Robins' first 1950 sessions were done in this way; their 'That's What The Good Book Says' was leased to Modern, and sold very well.

Leiber and Stoller then became involved with the L.A. label Spark, and concentrated their work upon it. The Robins, as their virtual protegees, went with them and had several excellent and quite successful singles on Spark, including 'Framed' and the famous 'Riot in Cell Block No. 9', which featured Richard Berry as a guest addition to the group, and is regarded today as one of the group's greatest recordings.

In 1955, Spark was taken over by Atlantic, Leiber and Stoller were contracted, and so were the Robins under their direction. Their 'Smokey Joe's Cafe' was issued on Atco, and towards the end of the year it entered the Top 100 to become their first pop hit. There was no Robins follow-up, however, because at this time either their producers or the executives at Atlantic decided a change of name was needed, and the group became the Coasters.

Success with the new name was not immediate. The first Coasters disc, 'Down In Mexico' sold only minimally, and the next, 'One Kiss Led To Another' was a very minor success. The group had to wait until the late Spring of 1957 to really make their mark with the gigantic double-sided hit 'Searchin''Young Blood'. Both sides of the record made the top 10: 'Young Blood', the initial success, going to No. 8, and then 'Searchin'' overtaking it to reach No. 5. The disc was a million-plus seller and both sides stayed in the Top 100 over six months; all the more surprising, then, that the follow-up 'Idol With The Golden 'Searching' overtaking it to reach struggled to reach No. 64 on the chart. This was to be the odd pattern of the Coasters' hit years: huge successes alternating with very minor hits or utter failures in a wierd seesaw fashion. It's hard to see why, for their productions never varied in quality, and their song lyrics, usually hilarious but wryly satirical of the U.S. scene of the 50's, were uniformly strong.

The next hit was 'Yakety Yak', in the spring of 1958. It reached No. 1, giving the group their second million seller and also breaking them in England, where it reached No. 12. 'The Shadow Knows' followed and flopped dismally and then along came the classic 'Charlie Brown', which swept the Coasters back to a U.S. No. 2, No. 5 in Britain, and a third gold disc.

1959 was the group's most consistently successful year. After 'Charlie Brown' they had another top tenner in 'Along Came Jones', and then yet another with 'Poison Ivy'. This latter was their fourth and final million-seller, and the last of their few hits in Britain, where it reached the bottom end of the Top 20. The flipside, 'I'm a Hog For You' was also very popular in the States, reaching No. 38 in its own right. It was about as successful as each side of the next single, 'What About Us' 'Run Red Run'.

By 1960, when the initial rock'n'roll boom was all but over and the group competition in the charts tremendous the Coasters began to find it harder going. 'Wake Me, Shake Me', 'Shoppin' For Clothes', now regarded as one of their classic sides, and a revival of the standard 'Besame Mucho' were all very minor hits, and it took a deliberate return to their rollocking 'Charlie Brown' style in mid-1961 with 'Little Egypt' to give them a final burst of chart glory. 'Egypt' reached No. 23, and then, apart from scraping to No. 96 with 'T'ain't Nothin' To Me', the Coasters were not to see the charts again.

In the mid-sixties, the group left Atlantic, and although they continued to perform as a live act in the U.S.A., sometimes as a soul attraction and occasionally on rock revival spots, they only made a couple of records, for CBS's soul label Date.

Recently, the Coasters signed for the King label, and were reunited with Leiber and Stoller, who produced for them an excellent revival of the Clovers' 'Love Potion No. 9'. Sadly, the record was not a success, but we should be hearing more of them.

The Coasters
BRITISH RELEASES TO 1960
+British Top 20 Hit
Singles

July 57 'Searchin', 'Young Blood' London 45HLE8450

Aug 58 'Yakety Yak', 'Zing Went The Strings Of My Heart' London 45HLE 8665+

Nov 58 'Sorry But I'm Gonna Have to Pass', 'The Shadow Knows' London 45HLE8729

Mar 59 'Charlie Brown', 'Three Cool Cats' London 45HLE8819+

June 59 'Along Came Jones', 'That Is Rock And Roll' London 45HLE8882

Sept 59 'I'm A Hog For You', 'Poison Ivy' London 45HLE8938+

Jan 60 'Run Red Run', 'What About Us' London 45HLE9020

Apr 60 'Besame Mucho' (Pts 1 and 2) London 45HLK9111

July 60 'Stewball', 'Wake Me Shake Me' London

Oct 60 'Shoppin' For Clothes', 'The Snake And The Bookworm' London 45

HLK9208

Dec 60 'Thumbin' A Ride', 'Wait A Minute' London 45HLK9293

LPs
1960 'Coasters Greatest Hits': 'Poison Ivy', 'Along Came Jones', 'Down in Mexico', 'The Shadow Knows', 'I'm A Hog For You', 'Charlie Brown', 'Yakety Yak', 'Zing Went The Strings Of My Heart', 'That Is Rock And Roll', 'Young Blood', 'Sweet Georgia Brown', 'Searchin'' London HAE2237

EDDIE COCHRAN

Eddie Cochran was born on 3rd October 1938 in Oklahoma, the youngest of five children. He started to teach himself guitar when he was twelve and by his mid-teens had developed into a very fine player. Unlike most white rock and roll singers of the fifties his guitar technique was such that he could have made a good living working as a session musician if he hadn't set out to become a star himself. He also played a little piano, bass and sax.

Eddie also differed from most other rock and rollers in the subject matter he chose to sing about:

'To hell with the phoney situations of Elvis, Haley, Lewis and Richards girls, Eddie didn't have time to worry about girls, he had a tough enough job staying alive. Every groove reeked with the misery of this two-bit punk, who had to work like hell to stay leader of his two-bit gang, in a two-bit town. If he crucified himself he earned a buck; if he behaved himself like an angel his dad lent him the car; if he waited at the corner he saw the girl he couldn't touch; but above all whatever he did, he did his way, and took orders from no-one'. (From an article on Eddie by Screamin' Steve in New Rockpile).

Shortly after he was born the Cochrans moved to Albert Lee, Minnesota, and in 1953 the family moved again to Southgate, California, and Eddie began working with one Hank Cochran, no relation, as the Cochran Brothers. The duo performed rockabilly and country and western material.

In 1955 Eddie met a songwriter called Jerry Capehart who was looking for someone to make demo tapes of his songs. The two teamed up, and made a series of tapes of Capehart's songs. At first Hank was in on the sessions but as the material became more rock and roll and less country and western the partnership coalesced into just Eddie and Jerry.

In late '55 Capehart started hawking the tapes round various record companies, and Eddie's first solo single was released that year: 'Skinny Jim'. It was put out on Crest records. During this period Eddie cut several other tracks for Crest and Ekko: 'Mr. Fiddle', 'Two Blue Singing Stars', 'Your Tomorrow May Never Come', 'Tired and Sleepy', 'Guilty Conscience', 'Half Loved', 'See Them Laugh', and 'Fools Paradise'.

Nothing much came of the Crest and Ekko recordings however, and in 1956 Capehart and Eddie secured a contract with a larger company, Liberty Records. The first single on this label was 'Sittin' In The Balcony'. Compared to Eddie's best records it was rather a mushy ballad, but it became his first hit.

At the same time as the first Liberty single, Eddie received a cameo role in the rock and roll movie ' The Girl Can't Help It'. He was seen singing a superb number, 'Twenty Flight Rock'. Visually he was pure dynamite and even today this filmed performance is very powerful. During the fifties Eddie also appeared in other movies: 'Go Johnny Go' with Chuck Berry, 'Untamed Youth', and 'Bop Girl'.

The second hit record was perhaps the best of all Eddie's releases: 'Summertime Blues', 1958. Like all his best material it dealt with the small but significant social realities of being a teenager in America in the fifties.

I'm gonna raise a fuss
I'm gonna raise a holler
About working all summer
Just to try to pull a dollar.
Well every time I call my baby,
Try to get a date,
My boss says 'No dice son,
You gotta work late'
Sometimes I wonder
What I'm gonna do,
But there ain't no cure
For the Summertime
For the summertime blues.

Well my mom and poppa told me
'Son you gotta make some money
If you wanna use the car
To go riding next Sunday'.
Well I didn't go to work,
Told the boss I was sick,
'Now you can't use the car,
'Cos you didn't work late'.
Sometimes I wonder
What I'm gonna do,
But there ain't no cure
For the summertime blues.

I'm gonna take two weeks,
Gonna have a fine vacation,
I'm gonna take my problem
To the United Nations.
Well I told my congressman,
He said 'Nope,
I'd like to help you son
But you're too young to vote'.
Sometimes I wonder
What I'm gonna do,
But there ain't no cure
For the summertime blues.

Summertime Blues
(Cochran/Capetart)
Cinephonic Music

Later that year Eddie had another hit with 'C'Mon Everybody', 'Well we'll really have

a party/ But we gotta put a guard outside'. Over the next two years he embarked on a series of backbreaking U.S. tours, tearing from town to town on one night stands. By all accounts he found the pace tiring and often spoke about settling down in California and concentrating on studio work. But he never did.

At the end of 1959 Eddie set out on his first European tour, which reached England at the beginning of 1960. He made his first British television appearance on ABC-TV's 'Boy Meets Girl'. His tour caused a sensation, both with the press and with the new rock and roll generation; it is said that George Harrison followed the tour round several cities. His last concert was at the Bristol Hippodrome on 16th April. The next day the car he was travelling in burst a tyre, skidded into a lampost and Eddie died in Somerset Hospital, Bath. Also in the car were Gene Vincent and Eddie's fiancée Sharon Sheeley. Records continued to be released after his death, and in Britain he had posthumous hits with 'Three Steps to Heaven', 1960 'Lonely', 1960, 'Weekend', 1961.

[Some of the details for this short biography come from Screamin' Steve's article on Eddie in New Rockpile. This is an excellent bi-monthly rock and roll magazine produced and edited by Eddie Muir and is well worth subscribing to if you have an interest in little known facts about fifties rock and roll stars. Subscription rates are 90p. for six issues, and you can order it from 152 Upper Lewes Road, Brighton, Sussex, BN2 3FB.]

BRITISH RELEASES TO 1960
+British Top 20 Hit
Singles

Apr 57	'Dark Lonely Street', 'Twenty Flight Rock' London 45HLU8386
July 57	'Completely Sweet', 'Sittin' In The Balcony' London 45HLU8433
Sept 58	'Love Again', 'Summertime Blues' London 45HLU8702+
Jan 59	'C'Mon Everybody', 'Don't Ever Let Me Go' London 45HLU8792+
June 59	'I Remember', 'Teenage Heaven' London 45HLU8880
Sept 59	'Boll Weevil', 'Something Else' London 45HLU 8944
Jan 60	'Hallelujah I Love Her So', 'Little Angel' London 45HLW9022
May 60	'Three Steps To Heaven', 'Cut Across Shorty' London 45HLG9115+
Oct 60	'Lonely', 'Sweetie Pie' London 45HLG9196+

EPs

1959	'C'Mon Everybody', 'Sitting In The Balcony', 'Twenty Flight Rock', 'Summertime Blues' London 1214
1959	'Something Else', 'Boll Weevil Song', 'Teenage Heaven', 'I Remember' London 1239
Mar 61	'Three Steps To Heaven', 'Cut Across Shorty', 'Jeannie Jeannie Jeannie', 'Pocketful Of Hearts' London 1262

LPs

1959	'Singin' To My Baby', 'Sittin' In The Balcony', 'Completely Sweet', 'Undying Love', 'I'm Alone Because I Love You', 'Lovin' Time', 'Proud Of You', 'Am I Blue', 'Twenty Flight Rock', 'Drive In Show', 'Mean When I'm Mad', 'Stockin's and Shoes', 'Tell Me Why', 'Have I Told You Lately That I Love You', 'Cradle Baby', 'One Kiss' London HA-U2093
1960	'Memorial Album': 'C'Mon Everybody', 'Three Steps To Heaven', 'Cut Across Shorty', 'Jeannie Jeannie Jeannie', 'Pocketful Of Hearts', 'Hallelujah I Love Her So', 'Don't Ever Let Me Go', 'Summertime Blues', 'Teresa', 'Something Else', 'Pretty Girl', 'Teenage Heaven', 'Boll Weevil Song', 'I Remember' London HAG2267

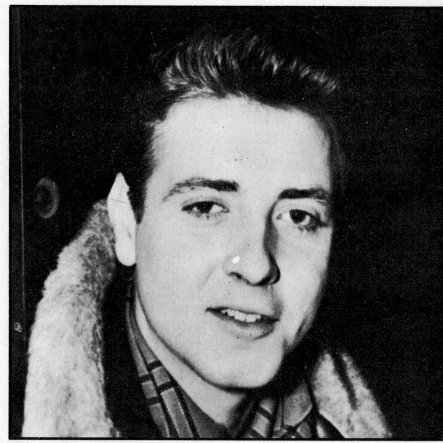

Eddie Cochran 1960

THE BEST RE-ISSUE AROUND
'Eddie Cochran'. United Artists Legendary Masters Series: UAD 60017/8 'Skinny Jim', 'Let's Get Together', 'Eddie's Blues', 'Little Lou', 'Pink Pegged Slacks', 'Jeannie Jeannie Jeannie', 'Something Else', 'Pretty Little Devil', 'Who Can I Count On', 'Thinkin' About You', 'Opportunity', 'Latch On', 'I'm Ready', 'Three Stars', 'Cotton Picker', 'Summertime Blues', 'Cut Across Shorty', 'Milk Cow Blues', 'My Way', 'Blue Suede Shoes', 'Nervous Breakdown', 'C'Mon Everybody', 'Sittin' In the Balcony', 'Twenty Flight Rock', 'Teenage Cutie', 'Hallelujah I Love Her So', 'Fourth Man Theme', 'Weekend', 'Boll Weevil', 'Long Tall Sally'

BO DIDDLEY

More than anything else Bo Diddley brought a mesmeric rhythm to rock music in the mid-fifties. The Bo Diddley beat, otherwise known as the 'tradesman's knock'. He didn't invent the beat, its probable origin is hundreds of years ago in Africa, but he was the first musician to use it commercially.

He has never had a big hit in Britain and has in fact been sadly ignored by the mass white audience in the U.S.A. and U.K. all his career. But he has influenced many musicians, and his influence was particularly strong during the British R&B revival of the early sixties. The Stones, The Yardbirds, The Animals, The Pretty Things, The Downliner Sect; they all owed as much to Bo as they did to anyone else.

He was born in McComb, Mississippi on 30th December 1928, an adopted child. His real parents were called Bates, but he took the name of the couple who adopted him and was called Elias McDaniel. In 1935, or thereabouts, the McDaniels moved to Chicago, where Bo acquired his nickname from his fellow school kids at Foster Vocational where he played trombone in the band. During this time he was also studying violin at the Ebeneezer Baptist Church.

It wasn't until he was 17 that he took up the guitar when he started playing gigs with a local R&B band. His first gig was at the 708 Club in Chicago. During this period he was also doing a bit of semi-pro boxing.

In 1955 he went to Chess Records who put him on their Checker label. 'Everybody else slammed the doors in my face' he has said. His first record was 'Bo Diddley' and introduced the Diddley beat. It was a big R&B hit and over the next few years Bo broke attendance records all over the States, notably at the Apollo in Harlem. His records too were consistently successful in the R&B charts. Most of them had much in common rhythmically and melodically, but they never got boring: 'Road Runner', Hey Bo Diddley', 'Diddley Daddy', 'Bo Diddley's a Gunslinger', 'You Can't Judge A Book By It's Cover', all great rock and roll tracks.

Many of the early records were given much of their appeal by Bo's marraccas-man Jerome,

and also his half-sister, the Duchess. Neither of them is still in the music business today; Jerome lives quietly in New York and the Duchess has had a baby.

A lot of other artists have used the Diddley beat; The Stones, Buddy Holly in 'Not Fade Away', Duane Eddy used it on 'Cannonball', Dee Clark for 'Hey Little Girl', Johnny Otis for 'Willie' and 'Hand Jive'.

He retained his position as a leading rock and roll artist till the early 1960s and since then has continued to play many club dates and make the occasional record. Phonogram have recently released an album of his Greatest Hits, see the record listing.

BRITISH RELEASES TO 1960
Singles

Sept 59	'Crackin' Up', 'Great Grandfather' London 45HLM8913
Oct 59	'Say Man', 'The Clock Strikes Twelve' London 45HLM8975
Oct 59	'Say Man, Back Again', 'She's Alright' London 45HL9035
Dec 59	'Road Runner', 'My Story' London 45HLM 9112

EPs

1957	'Bo Diddley', 'I'm A Man', 'Bring It To Jerome', 'Pretty Thing' London 1054

LPs

1960	'Go Bo Diddley', ' 'Crackin' Up', 'I'm Sorry', 'Bo's Guitar', 'Willie And Lillie', 'You Don't Love Me', 'Say Man', 'The Great Grandfather', 'Oh Yea', 'Don't Let It Go', 'Little Girl', 'Dearest Darling', 'The Clock Strikes Twelve' London HAM2230

THE BEST RE-ISSUE AROUND
'Bo Diddley's Golden Decade' Chess 6310 123. 'Bo Diddley', 'Bring It To Jerome', 'Hey Bo Diddley', 'Dearest Darling', 'I'm A Man', 'Diddley Daddy', 'Pretty Thing', 'She's Alright', 'You Can't Judge A Book By Its Cover', 'Road Runner', 'Say Man', 'I'm Sorry', 'Bo Diddley's A Gunslinger', 'I'm Looking for a Woman', 'Who Do You Love', 'Hush Your Mouth'

Bo Diddley 1957

FATS DOMINO

Fats was born in New Orleans on 10 May 1929. He started playing piano for dimes in bars when he was only ten, and even at this age had decided that he wanted to make his living as a musician. But when he left school family finances demanded Fats brought home more than the few pennies playing in bars was earning him so he got a job in a factory by day, while continuing to play in neighbourhood bars at night. While at the factory Fats was involved in an accident which damaged his hands so badly that doctors said he might never play piano again. In fact after two long years his hands had healed and he took a job with Dave Bartholomew's local dance combo.

The collaboration with Bartholomew was to last many years, with Bartholomew acting as songwriter/arranger and producer on many of Fats' most successful records. In 1949 they made their first, 'The Fat Man', backed by 'Detroit City Blues'. It was a very black sound and typically didn't receive any airplay outside of black radio stations. But it was a big hit in New Orleans, and by 1952 similar successes had made Fats the biggest performer and record seller on the local scene.

His music owed much to local New Orleans jump blues and boogie woogie, and was characterised by a front line of horns which played most of the riffs with instrumental solos being taken either by Fats on the piano or Herb Hardesty or Alvin Tyler on tenor sax. Fats rarely used a guitar on his early records and when one was used it was mixed well down.

National discovery came in 1954 after Lew Chudd, of Imperial Records, heard Fats and gave him a recording contract. The first big Imperial hit was 'Ain't it a Shame', in 1955, followed by 'Blueberry Hill', and these two releases established the Fat man as a major American rock and roller.

Fats stayed at the top till the end of the fifties, selling millions of records (he has had 18 million sellers, most of them during the early part of his career), and appearing in several rock and roll movies, like 'The Girl Can't Help It' and 'Disk Jockey Jamboree'.

By 1959 however Fats was losing popularity. The public then was perhaps even more fickle than it is today and few performers remained at the top for as long as Fats had done. It is also fair to say

that by that time the quality of his records was falling. Like many contemporary artists Fats had little say over what he recorded and much of the material from this period was maudlin rubbish quite unsuited to him or his original audience.

In 1962 the Imperial contract expired and was not renewed. Fats signed with ABC Paramount, moving shortly to Mercury where he remained until 1967. He continued to be fed weak material and his days as a star were definitely over, though he continued gigging almost every day of the year in clubs and roadhouses.

In 1968 he moved to Warner Brothers and the first album he recorded on that label was of the same quality as his early fifties releases. Unfortunately,

subsequent records were not up to that standard and he failed to make a comeback in any massive way. Today Fats is still working as many club dates as he wants, frequently appears in rock and roll revival shows, and lives very comfortably in New Orleans.

!!!Fats has now signed with Motown records; which must be good news.

BRITISH RELEASES TO 1960
+British Top 20 Hits
Singles

Feb 54	'Rosemary', You Said You Love Me' London HL8007
July 54	'Little School Girl','You Done Me Wrong' London 45HL8063
Nov 54	'Don't Leave Me This Way', 'Something's Wrong' London 45HL8096
Apr 55	'Don't You Hear Me Calling You', Love Me' London 45HL8124
June 55	'I Know' 'Thinking of You' London 45HL8133
Oct 55	'Ain't That a Shame', 'La-la' London 45HLU8173
May 56	'Boll Weevil', 'Don't Blame It On Me' London 45HLU8256
July 56	'I'm In Love Again', 'My Blue Heaven' London 45HLU8280+
Oct 56	'When My Dreamboat Comes Home', 'So Long' London 45HLU8309
Nov 56	'Blueberry Hill', I Can't Go On' London 45HLU8330+
Jan 57	'Don't Know You', 'Honey Chile' London 45HLU8356

Fats Domino in The Big Beat 1958

Feb 57   'Blue Monday', What's The Reason (I'm Not Pleasing You)' London 45HLP8377

May 57   'I'm In The Mood Love', 'I'm Walkin'' London 45HLP8407+

July 57   'It's You I Love', 'Valley Of Years' London 45HLO8449

Sept 57   'What Will I Tell My Heart', 'When I See You' London 45HLP8471

Dec 57   'I Still Love You', 'Wait and See' London 45HLP8519

Apr 58   'I Want You To Know', 'The Big Beat' London 45HLP8575+

June 58   'No No', 'Sick and Tired' London 45HLP8628

Aug 58   'Little Mary', 'Prisoners Song' London 45HLP8663

Nov 58   'It Must Be Love', 'Young School Girl' London 45HLP8727

Dec 58   'Coquette', 'Whole Lotta Lovin'' London 45HLP8759

Mar 59   'Telling Lies', 'When The Saints Go Marching In' London 45HLP8822

June 59   'I'm Ready', 'Margie' London 45HLP8865+

Sept 59   'I Want To Walk You Home', 'I'm Gonna Be A Wheel Someday' London 45HLP8942+

Dec 59   'Be My Guest', 'I've Been Around' London 45HLP9005+

Feb 60   'Country Boy', 'If You Need Me' London 45HLP9073+

May 60   'Tell Me That You Love Me', 'Before I Grow Too Old' London 45HLP9133

July 60   'Walkin' To New Orleans', 'Don't come Knocking' London 45HLP9163

Oct 60   'Three Nights A Week', Put Your Arms Around Me Honey' London 45HLP9198

Nov 60   'My Girl Josephine', Natural Born Lover' London 45HLP9244

EPs

1954   'You Said You Love Me', Rose Mary', 'Love Me', 'Don't You Hear Me Calling You' London 1022

1956   'My Blue Heaven', 'I'm In Love Again', 'So Long', When My Dreamboat Comes Home' London 1062

1957   'I'm Walking', 'Boll Weevil', 'I'm In the Mood For Love', 'Don't Blame It On Me' London 1079

1957   'The Rooster Song', 'My Happiness', 'As Time Goes By', 'Hey La Bas' London 1080

1957   'Carry On Rocking Pt. 1': 'The Fat Man', 'Tired Of Crying', 'Goin' Home', 'Goin' To The River' London 1115

1958   'Blueberry Hill' on compilation EP 'London Hit Parade Vol 2' London 1096

1958   'It's You I Love', 'Valley Of Tears', 'Where Did You Stay', 'Baby Please' London 1117

1958   'What Will I Tell My Heart', 'When I See You', 'Blue Monday', 'What's The Reason I'm Not Pleasing You'

London 1121

1958   'Wait and See', 'I Still Love You', 'The Big Beat', 'I Want You To Know', London 1138

1959   'The Rocking Mr. D Vol 1': 'Whole Lotta Lovin'', 'When The Saints Go Marchin' In', 'Telling Lies', 'Coquette' London 1206

1959   'The Rocking Mr. D Vol 2': 'Sick and Tired', 'Little Mary', 'Young School Girl', 'It Must Be Love' London 1207

LPs

1956   'My Blue Heaven', 'Swannee River Bop', 'Second Line Jump', 'Goodbye', 'Careless Love', 'I Love Her', 'I'm In Love Again', 'When My Dreamboat Comes Home', 'Are You Goin' My Way', 'If you Need Me' 'My Heart is In Your Hands', 'Fats Frenzy' London HAU2028

1957   'The Fat Man', 'Tired Of Crying', 'Goin' Home', 'You Said You Love Me', Goin' To The River', 'Please Don't Leave Me', 'Rose Mary', 'All By Myself', 'Ain't That A Shame', 'Poor Me', 'Boll Weevil', 'Don't Blame It On Me' London HAP2041

1957   'Detroit City Blues', 'Hide Away Blues', 'She's My Baby', 'Brand New Baby', 'Little Bee', 'Every Night About This Time', 'I'm Walkin'', 'I'm In The Mood For Love', 'Cheatin'', 'You Can

Pack Your Suitcase', 'The Fat Man', 'I'll Be Gone' London HAP2052

1958 'This Is Fats Domino': 'Blueberry Hill', 'Honey Chile', 'What's The Reason', 'Blue Monday', 'So Long', 'La La', 'Troubles Of My Own', 'You Done Me Wrong', 'Reeling and Rocking', 'The Fat Man's Hop', 'Poor Poor Me', 'Trust In Me' London HAP2073

1958 'This Is Fats': 'The Rooster Song', 'My Happiness', 'As Time Goes By', 'Hey La Bas', 'Love Me', 'Don't You Hear Me Calling You', 'It's You I Love', 'Valley Of Tears', 'Where Did You Stay', 'Baby Please', 'Thinking Of You', 'You Know I Miss You' London HAP2087

1959 'The Fabulous Mr. D': 'The Big Beat', 'I'll Be Glad When You're Dead You Rascal You', 'What Will I Tell My Heart', 'Barrel House', 'Little Mary', 'Sick And Tired', 'I Want You To Know', '44', 'Mardi Gras In New Orleans', 'I Can't Go On', 'Long Lonesome Journey', 'Young School Girl' London HAP2135

1960 'Let's Play Fats Domino': 'You Left Me', 'Ain't It Good', 'Howdy Podner', 'Stack & Billy', Would You', 'Margie', 'Hands Across The Table', 'The Samba', 'Ida Jane', 'Lil'

Liza Jane', 'I'm Gonna Be A Wheel Someday', 'I Want To Walk You Home' London HAP2223

'A Lot Of Dominoes': 'Put Your Arms Around Me Honey', 'Three Nights A Week', 'Shu-rah', 'Rising Sun', 'My girl Josephine', 'The Sheik Of Araby', 'Walkin' To New Orleans', 'Don't Come Knockin'', 'Magic Isles', 'You Always Hurt The One YOu Love', 'It's The Talk Of The Town', 'Natural Born Lover' London HAP2312

OTHER AMERICAN SINGLE RELEASES

The following singles were either not released in the U.K., or if they were only many years later on compilation albums. All were released in the U.S.A. on Imperial Records:

1950 'Boogie Woogie Baby', 'Little Bee'
1950 'Korea Blues', 'Every Night About This Time'
1951 'What's The Matter Baby', Tired Of Crying'
1951 'Don't You Lie To Me', 'Sometimes I Wonder'
1951 'Right From Wrong', 'No No Baby'
1951 'Rockin' Chair', 'Careless Love'
1952 'How Long', 'Dreamin''
1953 'Don't Leave Me This Way', 'Something's Wrong'
1954 'Little School Girl', 'You Done Me Wrong'
1954 'I Lived My Life', 'You Can Pack Your Suitcase'
1955 'Helping Hand', 'Don't You Know'

1958 'Yes My Darling', 'Don't You Know I Love You'

THE BEST RE-ISSUE AROUND

'Fats Domino'. United Artists Legendary Masters Series : UAD 60015/6

'The Fat Man', 'Hey La Bas', 'Going' Home', 'Please Don't Leave Me', 'Going' To The River', 'Ain't That a Shame', 'Poor Me', 'I'm In Love Again', 'When My Dreamboat Comes Home', 'Blueberry Hill', 'My Blue Heaven', 'The Rooster Song', 'I'm In The Mood For Love', 'Blue Monday', 'I'm Walkin'', 'It's You I Love', 'The Big Beat', 'Valley Of Tears', 'I Want You to Know', 'Whole Lotta Lovin', 'I Wanna Walk You Home', 'I'm Ready', 'Yes My Darling', 'I'm Gonna Be A Wheel Some Day', 'Walkin' To New Orleans', 'Be My Guest', 'I Hear You Knockin'', 'Let The Four Winds Blow'

DUANE EDDY

Duane was born in Corning, New York, on 26th April 1938. He moved with his family to Coolidge, Arizona, at the age of thirteen, having already played the guitar for some eight years. After leaving high school in 1954, he did some semi-professional playing at local clubs and dances, and became friendly with multi-instrumentalist Al Casey and also Lee Hazlewood, who was a disc-jockey on the local radio station KCKY as well as being as free-lance songwriter, music publisher and record producer. Duane played with Casey's group for a while, and also studied the guitar with jazz musician Jimmy Wybele. He developed the technique of playing on the bottom strings of the instrument to produce a deep twangy sound, and he and Hazlewood were not slow to recognise its commercial potential. A joint composition, 'Moovin' and Groovin', was recorded in Hazlewood's studio in Phoenix, and taken to Harry Finfer, President of Jamie Records in Philadelphia. The result was a recording contract and a Top 100 placing for 'Moovin' and Groovin' in the spring of 1958.

Duane gathered around him a recording group which he named The Rebels. They consisted of Al Casey on piano, Buddy Wheeler, bass, Steve Douglas, sax, Dorky Casey, rhythm, and Mike Bermani on drums; (this line-up changed over the years). Subsequently, records by Duane were usually billed: 'Duane Eddy, His Twangy Guitar, and The Rebels'.

The group's second disc was another Eddy-Hazlewood collaboration, titled 'Rebel Rouser'. It was a smash hit, reaching the U.S. Top 10 and the British Top 20, and selling over a million copies. 'Ramrod', an Al Casey tune, followed, and then 'Cannonball' and 'The Lonely One'. Duane had started on a long run of successes, all hard-hitting instrumentals with the distinctive twangy trademark, and almost all self-compositions in collaboration with Lee Hazlewood. He also began to appear on TV shows in the States, including Dick Clark's 'American Bandstand', and to headline concert performances and touring packages shows with a 'tour' version of the Rebels: Steve

Douglas, Ike Clanton and Mike Bermani.

In 1959, 'Cash Box' magazine awarded Duane its 'Outstanding Instrumentalist Of The Year' award, which the astonishing consistency, for a non-vocalist, of his disc sales certainly merited. During that year his chart positions had been: 'The Lonely One' : 23, 'Yep' : 30, 'The Quiet Three' : 46, 'Some Kinda Earthquake' : 37, 'First Love, First Tears' : 59. In England, he also had a top 5 smash with his version of the Henry Mancini-penned TV theme 'Peter Gunn'. This was the disc which really established Eddy in this country, and the one most closely associated with him to this day.

In 1960 the 'Cash Box' award was repeated, and Duane also won his second gold disc for 'Because They're Young'. This was the theme from the film of the same name, in which he also made his movie acting debut. The disc reached No. 3 in the U.S.A. and No. 2 in England, while further success came with 'Bonnie Came Back', 'Shazam', and 'Kommotion'. Duane also made

his first U.K. tour along with Bobby Darin, playing to packed houses and a welcome which was enthusiastic enough to justify extending his stay.

A second film part, in 'A Thunder Of Drums', came along in 1961, and two more film themes, 'Pepe' and 'Ring Of Fire', provided further hit records. However, Duane's singles were starting to lose their chart impact. After 'Pepe', No. 18, he couldn't raise another top 20 entry in the States, and by the time his contract had run its course at the end of 1961 he was failing to reach the top 100 at all. In Britain, too, the run of hits came to an end after a minor entry in September with 'Drivin' Home'. Duane and Lee Hazlewood, who was still co-writing and producing all his discs in Phoenix, did not lose heart, but sought a new outlet with a different company. A contract was signed with RCA-Victor, and the hits came once more. 'Deep In The Heart Of Texas' reached the lower half of the U.S. charts, and No. 19 in the U.K., and 'Ballad Of Paladin' returned Duane to the American Top 30 and the Top 10 here.

At about this time, Duane married Mirriam Johnson. It was also announced that he had sold 12 million discs to date; a number increased quickly to 13 by the success of his next single 'Dance With The Guitar Man'. This featured the innovation of a girl chorus named the Rebelettes, who chanted a vocal refrain throughout. Reactions to the girls' presence were mixed, but the record was a world-wide smash, reaching No. 12 in the U.S.A. and No. 3 in England, and winning a

Duane Eddy 1957

gold disc.

Unfortunately, the Rebelettes were thought to be such a good idea that Duane relentlessly stuck with them through a succession of mediocre instrumental/vocal follow-ups. 'Boss Guitar' was a top thirty hit, his last, on both sides of the Atlantic, but was widely condemned as poor quality material. After this, the public practically stopped buying, as non-classics like 'Your Baby's Gone Surfin'' and the desperate cash in 'Son Of Rebel Rouser' were consigned to oblivion.

Duane left RCA in 1965 and went through a succession of labels in the late sixties, like Colpix, Reprise, Congress and CBS. He made some fair discs like 'Trash' and 'Freight Train', but they aroused little interest: his commercial appeal had gone and so had his buying public. He last appeared on disc on 1971, playing a 'twangy guitar' cameo role on 'Rock And Roll Lullaby' by B. J. Thomas, but since then little has been heard of him.

BRITISH RELEASES TO 1960
+British Top 20 Hit
Singles

Sept 58   'Rebel Rouser',
          'Stalking ' London
          45HL8669+
Nov 58   'Ramrod', 'The Walker'
          London 45HL8723
Dec 58   'Cannonball', 'Mason
          Dixon Line' London
          45HL8764+
Sept 59   'Forty Miles Of Bad
          Road', 'The Bad Three'
          London HLW8929
Mar 59   'Detour' 'The Lonely
          One' London
          45HLW8821+
June 59   'Yep', 'Peter Gunn'
          London 45HLW8890+
Dec 59   'First Love First Tears',
          'Some Kinda
          Earthquake' London
          45HLW9007+
Feb 60   'Bonnie Come Back',
          'Movin' And Groovin'
          London 45HLW9050
Apr 60   'Shazam', 'Secret Seven'
          London 45HLW9104+
July 60   'Because They're
          Young', 'Rebel Walk'
          London 45HLW9162+
Nov 60   'Kommotion', 'Theme
          For Moon Children'
          London 45HLW9225+
          EPs
1958   'Rebel Rouser', 'The
          Walker', 'Stalkin ',
          'Ramrod' London 1175
1959   'Yep', 'Three-30 Blues',
          'Lonesome Road',
          'Lovin' You' London
          1217
1959   'Lonely One'
          'Cannonball', 'Detour',
          'Mason Dixon Line'
          London 1216
1960   'Because They're
          Young', 'Easy',
          'Shazam', 'Rebel Walk'
          London 1252
1960   'Up & Down', 'Lost

The Everly Brothers 1957

Island', 'You Are My
Sunshine', 'Blueberry
Hill' London 1257
          LPs
1960   'Especially For You':
          'Peter Gunn', 'Only
          Child', 'Lover', 'Fuzz',
          'Yep', 'Along The
          Navajo Trail', 'Just
          Because', 'Quiniela',
          'Trouble In Mind',
          'Tuxedo Junction',
          'Hardtimes', 'Along
          Came Linda' London
          HA-W2191
1959   'Have Twangy Guitar -
          Will Travel': 'The
          Lonesome Road', 'I
          Almost Lost My Mind',
          'Rebel Rouser',
          'Three-30 Blues',
          'Cannonball', 'The
          Lonely One', 'Detour',
          'Stalkin ', 'Ramrod',
          'Any Time', 'Movin'
          And Groovin', 'Loving
          You', London

HA-W2160
1960   'The Twang's The
          Thang': 'My Blue
          Heaven', 'Tiger Love
          And The Turnip
          Greens', 'The Last
          Minute Of Innocence',
          'Route No. 1', 'You Are
          My Sunshine', 'St. Louis
          Blues', 'Night Train To
          'The Battle', 'Trombone',
          'Blueberry Hill', 'Easy',
          'Rebel Walk', London
          HAW2236
1960   'Songs Of Our
          Heritage': 'Cripple
          Creek', 'Riddle Song',
          'John Henry', 'Streets
          Of Laredo', 'Prisoners
          Song', 'In The Pines',
          'Old Joe Clark',
          'Wayfaring stranger',
          'On Top Of Old
          Smokey', 'Mule Train',
          'Scarlet Ribbons'
          London HAW2285

22

THE EVERLY BROTHERS

The Everly Brothers were, and are, essentially country and western artists. Their vocal style, particularly their nasal close-harmony work, was strictly country, but they used a rock beat and their lyrics always dealt with teen subjects like parents and school and first crushes. Their's was one of the most distinctive sounds in rock in the fifties and early sixties and they have influenced countless other pop artists.

Don and Phil came from a performing country and western family. While still at school they toured with their parents Ike and Margaret, and did a regular radio show out of Brownie Kentucky called the Everly Family.

In 1956 their father saw the potential the two had to go it alone, and he succeeded in getting Chet Atkins in Nashville interested in them. It was Chet who obtained their first recording contract and generally gave them the initial push.

In 1956 they recorded and released their first single, 'Keep A Lovin' Me', 'The Sun Keeps On Shining', which failed to make the charts. The disc was for Columbia, and following its failure the Everlys moved to Cadence.

But their next single, 'Bye Bye Love' was a smash hit in the U.S.A. and Britain in 1957, and is still one of the best rock records of all time. From then on they got into the top of the charts with almost every release through to 1962: 'Wake Up Little Suzie', 'Claudette', 'Bird Dog', 'Love Of My Life', 'Lucille', 'Cathy's Clown', 'Walk Right Back', 'Temptation', were just some of them.

In 1958 they toured Britain for the first time with great success, and carried on visiting this country regularly.

The early sixties were difficult times for the Everlys though. First they both had to do time with the U.S. Marines, and when they went back on the road afterwards it was apparent that their personal relationship had deteriorated. Which was hardly surprising after all those years together on tour.

Their first major record label was Cadence: released by London over here in Britain. Then in 1960 they became the first signing to the new label Warner Brothers. The Everly Brothers are now with RCA and their old confederate Chet Atkins had produced an album for them.

The brothers are more together now than they have been for many years, and have regained much of their earlier popularity. They now concentrate on straight country material on record, but of course continue to give out with the old rock favourites in concert.

BRITISH RELEASES TO 1960
+British Top 20 Hit

Singles

July 57	'Bye Bye Love', 'I Wonder If I Care So Much' London 45HLA8440+
Nov 57	'Maybe Tomorrow', 'Wake Up Little Suzie' London 45HL8498+
Mar 58	'Should We Tell Him', 'This Little Girl Of Mine' London 45HLA8554
June 58	'All I Have To Do Is Dream', 'Claudette' London 45HLA8685+
Sept 58	'Bird Dog', 'Devoted To You' London 45HLA8685+
Jan 60	'Let It Be Me', 'Since You Broke My Heart' London 45HLA9039
July 60	'When Will I Be Loved', 'Be Bop A Lula' London 45HLA9157+
Dec 60	'Like Strangers', 'Leave My Woman Alone' London 45HLA9250+
Jan 60	'Always It's You', 'Cathy's Clown' Warner Bros. WB1+
May 60	'Lucille', 'So Sad', Warner Bros. 45WB19+
Dec 60	'Ebony Eyes', 'Walk Right Back' Warner Bros. 45WB33+

EPs

1957	'Bye Bye Love', 'I Wonder If I Care As Much', 'Wake Up Little Suzie', 'Maybe Tomorrow', London 1113
1958	'No. 2': 'This Little Girl Of Mine', Brand New Heartache', 'Keep A Knockin', 'Be Bop A Lula' London 1148
1958	'No. 3': 'Rip It Up', 'Leave My Woman Alone', 'Should We Tell Him', 'Hey Doll Baby' London 1149
1958	'No. 4': 'All I Have To Do Is Dream', 'Claudette', 'Bird Dog', 'Devoted To You' London 1174
1959	'Songs Our Daddy Taught Us Pt. 1': 'Rovin Gambler', 'Down In The Willow Garden', 'Long Time Gone', 'Lightning Express' London 1196

1959   'Pt. 2': 'That Silver Haired Daddy Of Mine', 'Who's Gonna Shoe Your Pretty Little Feet', 'Barbara Allen', 'So Many Years', London 1196

1959   'Pt. 3': 'I'm Here To Get My Baby Out Of Jail', 'Rockin' Alone In An Old Rockin' Chair', 'Kentucky', 'Put My Little Shoes Away' London 1197

1960   'Problems', 'Love Of My Life', 'Take A Message To Mary', 'Poor Jenny' London 1229

LPs

1958   'This Little Girl Of Mine', 'Maybe Tomorrow', 'Bye Bye Love', 'Brand New Heartache', 'Keep A Knockin ', 'Be Bop A Lula', 'Rip It Up', 'I Wonder If I Care as Much', Wake Up Little Suzie', 'Leave My Woman Alone', 'Should We Tell Him', 'Hey Doll Baby' London HAA2081

1959   'Songs Our Daddy Taught Us': 'Roving Gambler', 'Down In The Willow Garden' 'Long Time Gone', 'Lightning Express', 'That Silver Haired Daddy Of Mine', 'Who's Gonna Shoe Your Pretty Little Feet', 'Barbara Allen', 'Oh So Many Years', 'I'm Here To Get My Baby Out Of Jail', 'Rockin' Alone In An Old Rockin' Chair', 'Kentucky', 'Put My Little Shoes Away'

Adam Faith 1959

London HA-A2150

1960   'It's Everly Time': 'So Sad', 'Just In Case', 'Memories Are Made Of This', 'That's What You Wanna Do To Me', 'Sleepless Nights', 'What Kind Of Girl Are You', 'Oh True Love', 'Some Sweet Day', 'Nashville Blues', 'You Thrill Me', 'I Want You To Know' Warner Bros. WS8012

1960   'The Fabulous Style Of The Everly Brothers': 'Like Strangers', 'All I Have To Do Is Dream', 'Claudette', 'Oh What A Feeling', 'Take A Message To Mary',

'Devoted To You', 'When Will I Be Loved', 'Bird Dog', 'Till I Kissed You', 'Problems', 'Poor Jenny', 'Love Of My Life' London HAA2266

1960   'A Date With The Everly Brothers': 'Made To Love', 'That's Just Too Much' 'Stick With Me Baby', 'Baby What You Want Me To Do', 'Sigh Cry Almost Die', 'Always It's You', 'Love Hurts', 'Lucille', 'So How Come No-one Loves Me', 'Donna Donna', 'A Change Of Heart', 'Cathy's Clown' Warner Bros. WS8028

ADAM FAITH

Adam started life as Terence Nelhams in Acton, London, on 23rd June 1940. As a teenager his ambition was to become a film editor, and he started work in the Movie industry as a messenger boy at Rank Screen Services. He enjoyed singing as a sideline, though, and with some workmates formed a skiffle group known as the 'Worried Men', which performed on an amateur basis around many of the coffee bars in Soho: including the famous '2 I's', scene of many star finds . It was here that T.V. producer Jack Good saw the group. The 'Worried Men' didn't impress him too much, but their lead singer did, and Jack suggested that Adam should pursue a solo career.

It was not easy at first. Adam made a couple of records for Top Rank which caused little reaction, and also did some T.V. appearances, again without any great success. Discouraged, he returned to the cutting studios at Rank, and probably would have stayed there had it not been for John Barry, whom Adam had met and become friendly with during his earlier unsuccessful period. John had been booked for the new T.V. show 'Drumbeat', and called Adam to tell him that the show's producer was looking for a beat singer who had not had much previous T.V. exposure. Adam was auditioned, signed, and became resident on 'Drumbeat' for over five months. He also got a part in the film 'Beat Girl', which was fairly successful.

On 'Drumbeat' Adam met songwriter Johnny Worth, who suggested that he needed to switch from hard rock material if he wanted to have a hit record, and offered Adam one of his own songs, 'What Do You Want?'.

The record was released on Parlophone, to which Adam had been newly contracted. With an arresting John Barry pizzicato string backing and a Buddy Holly-ish styling from Adam which included his soon-to-be-famous 'bye-bee' pronunciation of the word 'baby', plus an extremely strong hook-line. Released in November 1959, it raced up the charts in the short space of three weeks, to reach No. 1 and sell over a quarter-of-a-million copies. Adam finished 1959 as a major bill-topping star.

During 1960, nobody but Cliff Richard could match Adam's astonishing run of disc successes. A whole flood of Johnny Worth compositions wrapped in John Barry's string arrangements tore the charts apart. 'Poor Me' went to No. 1, 'Someone Else's Baby', or 'bye-bee', to 2, and 'Made You', 'How About That' and the Christmassy 'Lonely Pup' into the Top 5. Adam made a second film, the comedy 'Never Let Go' with Peter Sellers, and also appeared in the Royal Variety Show, as well as topping the bill on tours and T.V. shows. 1961 provided more of the same, with more hits in 'Who Am I?', 'Easy Going Me', 'Don't You Know It?' and 'The Time Has Come', another quarter-million seller, and another successful film in 'What A Whopper!', an unbelievable comedy about the Loch Ness Monster.

1962 saw the beginning of Adam's attempts to broaden his showbiz horizons. He wanted to get into dramatic acting, and took a serious part in the film 'Mix Me A Person'. He also attempted a wider range of material on record; the melancholy ballad 'Lonesome' showed a completely new vocal side, and on 'Don't That Beat All', he dispensed with the usual John Barry accompaniment in favour of a new arrangement by Johnny Keating. His other hits for the year, however, 'As You Like It' and 'Baby Take A Bow', were more in his accepted style, and kept his old fans happy.

As the sixties moved on and the Beatles burst onto the music scene, with the group boom mushrooming behind them, times suddenly became harder for the earlier established soloists. At first Adam was one of those to suffer. His earlier 1963 hits 'What Now' and 'Walkin' Tall' failed to register anything like as strongly as his previous successes, and a rethinking of musical policy was obviously called for. Adam's answer was to get himself a group in the new idiom the Roulettes, and he immediately had a top 5 hit with the Mersey-beat-styled 'The First Time', closely followed by the almost equally successful 'We Are In Love' and a lesser hit in 'If He Tells You'. After this, however, he dropped out of the running for a while behind a flood of newer pop names, and didn't re-emerge until the very end of 1964 with what was to be his last major success, 'A Message To Martha'. Back in a ballad style once more this was a cover version of a Bacharach/David number originally recorded by Lou Johnson. It climbed to No. 9 during Christmas week, and after it dropped out of the charts, Adam only made the top 30 once more with 'Stop Feeling Sorry For Yourself'.

At the same time, Adam had his only hit in the U.S.A., of all things, with one of his B-sides, 'It's Alright'. This was at a time when practically anything British stood a good chance if promoted in the States, and this number obviously carried enough of an echo of Merseybeat to attract transatlantic ears; at least, enough to carry it to No. 30 in their Top 100, in January 1965.

In the years since that time, Adam has made his reputation chiefly through his acting, having fulfilled his earlier stated desire to develop as a dramatic performer. Recently, of course, he won a mass following all over again with his 'Budgie' T.V. series. He never entirely turned his back on records, however, and has occasionally broken with minor chart successes.

Alan Freed

BRITISH RELEASES TO 1960
+British Top 20 Hit

Singles

1957	'Brother Heartache and Sister Tears' HMV 45POP438
1958	'Country Music Holiday', 'High School Confidentail' HMV 45POP557
1959	'Ah Poor Little Baby', 'Runk Bunk' Top Rank 45JAR126
1959	'From Now Until Never', 'What Do You Want' Parlophone 45R4591+
1960	'Poor Me', 'The Reason' Parlophone 45R4623
1960	'Big Time', 'Someone Else's Baby' Parlophone 45R4643+
1960	'Made You', 'What The Devil' Parlophone 45R4665+
1960	'How About That', 'With Open Arms' Parlophone 45R4689+
1960	'Greenfinger' 'Lonely Pup' Parlophone 45R4708+
	'This Is It', 'Who Am I' Parlophone 45R4735+

EPs

1959	Included on BBCTV Drumbeat EP, Fontana 17146, with the song 'I Vibrate'
1960	'Adam's Hit Parade': 'What Do You Want', 'Poor Me', 'Someone Else's Baby', 'Johnny Comes Marching Home', Parlophone 8811
1960	'Adam': 'Wonderful Time', 'Diamond Ring', 'Summertime', 'Greenfinger' Parlophone 8824

LPs

1960	'Adam': 'Wonderful Time', 'Diamond Ring', 'Summertime', 'Greenfinger', 'Piper Of Love', 'A Girl Like You', 'Turn Me Loose', 'So Many Ways', 'Singing In The Rain', 'Fare Thee Well My Pretty Maid', 'I'm A Man', 'Hit The Road To Dreamland' Parlophone PMC1128

ALAN FREED

Alan Freed is often referred to as the father of rock'n'roll, and in fact it was he who coined the phrase. He played a vital part in the early 1950's in bringing this new form of rhythm and blues to the public, and in doing so became part of the legend.

Freed was born in Johnstown, Pennsylvania on 15th December 1922. He entered radio at the age of seventeen, working on the station at Ohio State College while he was studying engineering there. At the start of the second world war, he was drafted into the signal corps, but served only a few months before coming down with double Mastoiditis. A period of intensive treatment followed, and then a medical discharge from the service in 1942. The infection had partially impaired his hearing, and for the rest of his life Freed was deaf to certain sounds.

Freed returned to his studies, getting his engineering degree in 1943, but then went straight to work in radio as an announcer at WKST Ohio. He became a disc jockey in 1945, while working on another Ohio station, WAKR. The story goes that he filled in one night when the regular jock failed to turn up, made an immediate impression upon listeners and management, and was given a programme contract the next day.

It was when he went to work for station WJW in Cleveland, that Freed's popularity really began to mushroom. He became aware of the growing popularity amongst listeners for the rhythm and blues records which were made for the black audience. They were supposed not to have any appeal to whites, but Freed had noticed how much white teenagers enjoyed dancing to them, and recognised the possibility of a whole unsuspected mass market. He began to play more and more R&B discs on the air, and an ever-widening audience of blacks and whites began to listen to what he called 'rock and roll' music. This catch phrase came from the lyric of an old R&B hit; Freed thought it summed up the sound and rhythm of the music pretty well, and he used it so often that it became a sort of trade mark, along with his habit of joining in with his favourite records by thumping out the rhythm on an old phone book while the disc was playing.

In March 1952, with his WJW radio show 'The Moondog Rock'n'Roll Party' a raging success, Freed decided to promote a rock'n'roll stage show. He booked the Cleveland Arena, which had a capacity of 10,000 and found himself faced with a virtual riot when upwards of 30,000 people arrived and tried to get in. The show was cancelled and should have been a financial disaster, but as Freed later put it: 'Everyone had such a grand time breaking into the arena, that they didn't ask for their money back'. Nevertheless, he risked no more similar events, and concentrated on sit-down shows in theatres. Every one was a sell-out success.

A year later, at the peak of his popularity, a serious car smash put Freed out of commission for an extended period. Only after a long series of operations and plastic surgery, did he return to broadcasting. The New York station WINS offered him a job with a yearly salary of 25,000 dollars, and Freed took his rock'n'roll show there on the 8th September 1954.

Freed's popularity rose to new heights in New York via radio and further stage shows and rock'n'roll dances. As rock grew to national and then international proportions, the man who had been with it from the beginning stayed in the forefront, with radio programmes and package shows which brought rock and roll to the whole of America. Little Richard, Chuck Berry, Fats Domino, Jerry Lee Lewis and scores more appeared on his shows. He also starred in several films, most of which were canned versions of his stage shows, and featured rock'n'roll stars performing their latest or greatest hits. All were wildly successful, and to this day the titles are fondly remembered: 'Rock Around The Clock', 'Don't Knock The Rock', 'Go Johnny Go', 'Rock, Rock, Rock', and 'Mister Rock'n'Roll'.

Freed's bubble finally burst in 1960, when the payola storm burst across the U.S. entertainment world. As official investigations turned up nationwide bribery and corruption, careers began to tumble on all sides, with the disc jockeys taking the hardest rap of all; Freed amongst them. As one of the biggest, he had farthest to fall: he was fired from all his radio and T.V. shows, and practically made the scapegoat for the whole payola 'scandal'. Angered by this excessive treatment, he left New York and went to a second-string Los Angeles station, KDAY. Then he took up drinking, which accelerated his slide through a

Billy Fury 1959

succession of progressively minor jobs into relative obscurity. He was never again to find his star status or his once infallible streak of success. Finally, on 20th January 1965, at Palm Springs, California, Freed died of uremia.

Freed's story in many ways is one of rock's tragedies, as he was one of those who eventually fell victim to the thing which they had been instrumental in creating. Nevertheless, rock'n'roll, and everything in pop music which has developed from it, undoubtedly owes a debt to this man who was its potential from the very beginning. He opened up white acceptance of black music, and paved the way for and pushed forward the performers and writers of R&B and Rock'n'Roll, at a time when the established record industry resented them, and the mass public was simply unaware of them.

BRITISH RELEASES TO 1960
  Singles
1957 'Right Now Right Now', 'Teen Rock' Vogue Coral 45Q72219
1957 'Rock'n'Roll Boogie', 'Teeners Canteen' Vogue Coral 45Q72230
  LPs
1957 'Rock and Roll Party': 'Right Now Right Now', 'Only You', 'Up And Down', 'Rock Around The Clock', 'Slow Boat to Monaca', 'Rock'n'roll Boogie', 'Ten Rock', 'See You Later Alligator', 'Teeners Canteen', 'The Great Pretender', 'The Grey Bear', 'Take One', (with the Modernaires and Hal and Al) Vogue Coral CVA9033
1958 'Swell', 'Sometimes I'm Happy', 'John Thompson', 'Twenty One', 'Sure', 'Sentimental Journeys', 'Easy Rock', 'Stop Look And Run' Vogue Coral CVA9066

N.B. All recordings by 'The Alan Freed Rock And Roll Band'.

BILLY FURY

Ronald Wincherley was born in Liverpool on 17th April 1941. His parents lived in the tough Dingle area of the city, and he did not have an easy childhood: he suffered from delicate health and frequent bouts of rheumatic fever, and was once almose knifed to death by a local gang.

He was working on a Mersey tugboat when in October 1958 he saw a poster advertising Larry Parnes' Rock extravaganza at the Birkenhead Essoldo. Appearing backstage at the cinema with his guitar, he demanded point blank to see Parnes for an interview, and sang one of several songs he'd composed and sung with some of his mates on the tugboat, 'Maybe Tomorrow'. Parnes, who had been immediately impressed by the boy's nerve, was doubly so when he heard him sing. Ron was immediately added to the Birkenhead bill, where he sang and played a couple of his songs with amazing reaction from the audience. This was all the confirmation Larry Parnes needed that he had found a new star.

Within a month, Ron had been renamed Billy Fury and had signed a recording contract with Decca. 'Maybe Tomorrow' was issued on a single, and entered the top 20 early in 1959, to be followed over the next couple of years by 'Margo Don't Go', 'Colette', both self-compositions, 'That's Love' and 'Wondrous Place'. Billy toured the country on the Parnes extravaganza and soon developed a stage act comparable with Elvis Presley's, to a similar tide of protest from adults screaming about the 'corruption of youth'. The criticism became so intense, in fact, that Billy finally announced publicly, on the advice of his father, that he was 'cleaning up' the act. This allowed T. V. to show the whole of him on the scree screen; previously, despite his becoming a regular on 'Oh Boy', followed by 'Boy Meets Girls' and 'Wham', producers had followed a habit of screening him, again like Presley, only from the waist up.

In 1961, Billy made the transition from rock star to teenage idol, largely by switching, as Cliff Richard before him, to dramatic beat-ballads on his

records. A cover version of Tony Orlando's 'Halfway To Paradise' midway through the year catapulted him into the top 10 for the first time, reaching No. 4 and enjoying no less than a five-month stay in the charts. It was swiftly followed by a revival of 'Jealousy' and another Orlando cover 'I'd Never Find Another You', both of which made the top 5. In 1962, he tried a brief switch to an R&B style with a cover of Gladys Knight's 'Letter Full Of Tears' which puzzled the untutored British ears of the time, and only reached No. 17. Then it was back to the best ballads and huge success with 'Last Night Was Made For Love', 'Once Upon A Dream', 'Because Of Love', a Presley cover, something few people could have got away with at the time, 'Like I've Never Been Gone', 'When Will You Say I Love You', and 'In Summer'. Most of these were quarter-million sellers; Billy was second only to Cliff Richard in national popularity, and his weekly earnings were in the four-figure bracket.

At this time, Billy also made his feature film, a song-packed

opus entitled 'Play It Cool'. While no great thespian achievement, it was extremely successful. An E.P. of songs from it sold incredibly well, and the hit 'Once Upon A Dream also came from the soundtrack.

Billy's star status and disc sales only began to falter, and then only slightly, towards the end of 1963, with the sudden upsurge of Beatle mania. As 'In Summer' left the charts, 'Somebody Else's Girl', a song of no less quality, only just scraped the twenty. Like many other 'established' stars, Billy had to find really strong material to grab the ears of the Merseybeat freaks. He came up with a trio of American revivals/ covers in 'Do You Really Love Me Too'. 'I Will'/'Nothin' Shakin', and 'It's Only Make Believe'. His powerful treatment took this latter Conway Twitty classic to No. 10 in the charts while the Beatles were topping with 'A Hard Day's Night'.

So Billy endured through 1964, and started 1965 off equally strongly with another typical ballad called 'I'm Lost Without You'. But times were becoming harder for soloists as the sixties group explosion continued and other new styles made their arrival. Billy eventually went down with the rest, after a final 1965 stab at the top ten with 'In Thoughts Of You', a best-forgotten second film called 'I Gotta Horse'; he did have one, too, Anselmo, which came fifth in the Derby; and a good fade-out of top thirty hits in 'Run To My Lovin' Arms', 'I'll Never quite Get Over You' and 'Give Me Your Word'.

Billy went into the club and

Bill Haley arriving in London 1957

cabaret circuit and continued to make discs which sold reasonably, changing labels late in the 60's from Decca to Parlophone, and eventually forming his own Fury label a couple of years ago. He recently made a comeback performing in the film 'That'll Be The Day', as a late-50's rocker closely based on himself. He even brought back his old stage act into it, and nobody now will bat an eyelid.

BRITISH RELEASES TO 1960
+British Top 20 Hit
Singles
1959　'Gonna Type A Letter', 'Maybe Tomorrow' Decca 45F11102+
1959　'Don't Knock Upon My Door','Margo Don't Go' Decca 45F11128
1959　'Angel Face', 'Time Has Come' Decca 45F11158
1959　'My Christmas Prayer', 'The Last Kiss' Decca 45F11189
1960　'Baby How I Cried', 'Colette' Decca 45F11200+
1960　'That's Love', 'You Don't Know' Decca 45F11237+
1960　'Alright Goodbye', 'Wondrous Place' Decca 45F11267
1960　'A Thousand Stars', 'Push Push' Decca 45F11311
EPs
1959　'Margo', 'Don't Knock Upon My Door', 'Maybe Tomorrow', 'Gonna Type A Letter' Decca 6597
LPs
1960　'The Sound Of Fury': 'That's Love', 'My Advice', 'Phone Call', 'You Don't Know' 'Since You've Been Gone', 'Turn My Back On You', 'Don't Say It's Over', 'It's You I Need', 'Alright Goodbye This Way' Decca LF1329
1960　'Gonna Type A Letter', 'Maybe Tomorrow', 'Don't Knock Upon My Door', 'Time Has Come', 'Colette', 'Baby How I Cried', 'Angel Face', 'Wondrous Place', 'Last Kiss' Decca ACL1047

BILL HALEY

Bill Haley and the Comets were the first group to reach international stardom through rock'n'roll, and Haley, in a sense, was the first rock teenage idol, even if he wasn't a teenager.

Bill was born in Highland Park, Michigan, and spent most of his youth in Wilmington in Delaware. Musically inclined from a very early age, he had learned to play the guitar before he was in his teens, and by the age of 13 was entertaining publically in the local area, first solo and then with a small country band which he had formed with schoolfriends.

At fifteen, Bill left home and spent several years on he road. He worked where he could, and played and sang with various itinerant C&W bands and travelling roadshows. After some valuable experience with an outfit known as the Down homers, Bill decided to form his own band, during the late 40's.

The band, known as Bill Haley's Saddlemen, was formed in Pennsylvania, primarily as a Country outfit. They played regular club dates in and around Philadelphia together with broadcasts over some of the city's stations; Bill himself was also a radio station music director for part of this period. Eventually, they came to cut some records in the C&W idiom, but none sold particularly well. Bill then began to experiment with the band's sound, bringing in a strongly amplified electric guitar and a more pronounced regular beat from the bass and drums, to develop a rhythmic style more in the manner of the black jump blues bands than a conventional country combo. Simultaneously, their repertoire began to make more than a passing glance at R&B tunes; their 'Rocket 88', made in 1951, was actually an adaptation of a number which was already big in the specialist R&B market in its original version by Jackie Brenston.

By 1953, Bill and the group were recording for the Essex label and as if to emphasise the casting off of their C&W had changed their name to 'Bill Haley and the Comets'. They cut one of Bill's own songs, 'Crazy Man Crazy', in a strong beat-accented style, and midway through the year it climbed into the national top 20. The disc was quite a breath of fresh air amidst the croonings and whimperings which tended to clog the charts of the time, and immediately the young white audience which had already been curiously sampling R&B items from the likes of the Orioles and Fats Domino latched onto the Comets. The large Decca label noticed the growing interest, and signed the group from Essex to record rock'n'roll.

Bill cut his two most famous and influential numbers at his very first Decca session, on 12th April 1954: 'Shake, Rattle And Roll' and 'Rock Around The Clock'. The former was a cover of a big R&B hit by Joe Turner, but the latter was a new song, destined to be the first and biggest-selling rock song of them all. 'Clock', issued in the early summer, did not sell astoundingly well at first, but 'Shake', issued as a quick follow-up, took the group back into the U.S. top 20 in September. It shot into the top 5, stayed there practically until Christmas, and went over the million sales mark. Bill and the Comets were suddenly bill-topping stars.

Early in 1955, the film 'The Blackboard Jungle' was released in the U.S.A., and featured 'Rock Around The Clock' heavily in its sound-track, triggering off a wave of enthusiasm for the number. It went into the charts in April and raced to No. 1 and an immediate gold disc, remaining in the Top 100 and selling in its thousands through until December, while 'Dim Dim The Lights', 'Mambo Rock', 'Razzle Dazzle', and the double sided smash 'Burn That Candle', 'Rock-A-Beatin' Boogie' burned in and out of the charts in its wake. Bill and the group were now received in concert with a near-hysterical reception which had previously only been afforded heart-throb balladeers Frank Sinatra and Johnny Ray. Bill's kiss curl hanging over his forehead and the instrument-mounting and playing-lying-on-their-backs antics of the Comets were exulted as symbols of the new music of youth.

The group first broke in Britain at the end of 1954, with 'Shake, Rattle And roll' and 'Rock Around The Clock' entering the U.K. top 20 almost simultaneously. Once again the former disc was the most immediately successful, climbing to No. 4 while 'Clock' languished in the second ten and then faded away. 'Mambo Rock' provided a third hit in April, and then in the Autumn, with 'The Blackboard Jungle' on British release, interest in 'Rock Around The Clock' was startlingly rekindled here as it has been in the U.S.A., and the record bounded to a long stay at No. 1, lasting well into the New Year.

1956 saw no let-up in

Haleymania, despite the appearance on the scene of a real teen idol, in the sense that he was a teenager himself, in the form of Elvis Presley, whose 'Heartbreak Hotel' topped the American charts in April. Bill started the year in the U.S. with 'See You Later Alligator', which rapidly shot to No. 6 in the chart and provided him with his third gold disc. Then came a flurry of double-sided hits in 'R-o-c-k', 'The Saints Rock And Roll', 'Hot Dog Buddy Buddy', 'Rockin' Through The Rye', and 'Rip It Up', 'Teenager's Mother', and to round off the year, 'Rudy's Rock', featuring the talents of saxman Rudi Pompilli, one of the original Comets who is still playing with Haley to this day.

In England, which was somewhat slow to accept Elvis, Bill's discs hit the charts even harder. 'Rock-A-Beatin' Boogie' went to No. 4, 'See You Later Alligator' to No. 7, 'The Saints Rock'n'roll' to 5, 'Rockin' Through The Rye' to 3, 'Razzle Dazzle' to 13, re-entries by 'Clock' and 'Alligator' to 5 and 12 respectively on the second innings, and finally 'Rip It Up' to No. 4. It was a most convincing show of chart supremacy; all the more amazing therefore that before 1957 was more than a few months old, Bill and the Comets should suddenly tumble from favour.

The year started off in fine style, with a Haley tour of England. This had followed hard on the heels of the U.K. cinema release of the Alan Freed film 'Rock Around The Clock', in which Bill and the Band were featured, and British rock fans were in a flurry of eager anticipation. The Comets arrived to a tumultuous welcome and scenes of great excitement at their early concerts, but as the tour progressed the furore died down

somewhat, and Bill's final departure from the country was a quiet, almost anonymous one. Haleymania, in Britain at least, appeared to have burned itself out. It was reflected in the charts, too; a re-released oldie from the Essex days, 'Rock The Joint', had a brief run in the top 20, and was swiftly followed by the title song from the Comets' second feature film, which was expected to do at least as well as their previous year's smashes. However, 'Don't Knock The Rock' burst in coincidentally with the start of Bill's tour and went to No. 7, but within two months had vanished again from the charts, taking with it the name of Bill Haley and the Comets. They did have a U.K. hit again during the late 60's, when there was a resurgence of interest in rock and roll.

The band's decline in America was slower but just as sure. They had just two hits in 1957 with 'Forty Cups Of Coffee' and 'Billy Goat', and neither got more than halfway up the Hot 100, although the 'Don't Knock The Rock' film did good business. In 1958 they scored with 'Skinny Minnie', and in 1959 with 'Joey's Song', and then it was the end of the chart road.

Theories about the comparatively sudden burst of the Haley bubble are quite well formulated. Firstly, Bill was not young and neither was he glamorous, and it was not long before rock'n'roll had thrown up new idols who were both, and therefore had much stronger teen appeal. Secondly, his music was plain predictable. His discs were very similar to one another rhythmically, they had the same booting off-beat and the sax and guitar breaks in the same places, and the same bland vocals on lyrics which were often as not about rock'n'roll and nothing else. Too much familiarity in such profusion led inevitably to overkill.

Bill did not give up performing when major success slipped away. In fact, he carried on playing, and recording, in much the same style throughout the 60's and right up to the present day. The line-up of the Comets changed several times, but they went into the lucrative U.S. club circuit which brought in a comfortable living. The British rock'n'roll revival of 1968 brought them back here for another tour, which was highly successful, to the extent that 'Rock Around The Clock' actually

Bill Haley on stage with The Comets at the Dominion, Tottenham Court Road 1957

re-entered the U.K. top 30. Since then the subsequent 'revival' boom in America has seen them on several golden oldies packages, and in the Rock'n'Roll Revival Spectaculars organised by Richard Nader. They played at the Wembley Rock Restival in the summer of 1972, and were one of the hits of the show. And it's a sobering thought to realise that Haley has probably played 'Rock Around The Clock' and 'Shake Rattle And Roll' on every working day for the last 19 years.

BRITISH RELEASES TO 1960
+British Top 20 Hit

Singles

1953 'Patacake', 'Fractured' London C1216
1955 'ABC Boogie', 'Shake Rattle And Roll' Brunswick 45-0-5338+
1955 'Thirteen Women', 'Rock Around The Clock' Brunswick 45-0-5317+
1955 'Dim Dim The Lights', 'Happy Baby' Brunswick 45-0-5373
1955 'Birth Of The Boogie', 'Mambo Rock' Brunswick 45-0-5405+
1955 'Green Tree Boogie', 'Sundown Boogie' London 45HL8142
1955 'Farewell So Long Goodbye', 'I'll Be True' London 45HLF8161
1955 'Rocking Chair On The Moon', 'Ten Little Indians' London 45HLF8194
1956 'Burn That Candle', 'Rock A Beatin' Boogie' Brunswick 45-0-5509+
1956 'Paper Boy', 'See You Later Alligator' Brunswick 45-0-5530+
1956 'R-o-c-k', 'The Saints Rock And Roll' Brunswick 45-0-5565+
1956 'Hot Dog Buddy Buddy', 'Rockin' Through The Rye' Brunswick 45-0-5582+

1956 'Razzle Dazzle', 1956 'Two Hound Dogs' Brunswick 45-0-5453+
1956 'I'm Gonna Dry Every Tear With A Kiss'. 'Why Do I Cry Over You?' Melodisc 1376
1956 'Rip It Up', 'Teenagers Mother' Brunswick 45-0-5615+
1957 'Blue Comet Blues', 'Rudy's Rock' Brunswick 45-0-5616
1957 'Rock The Joint', 'Yes Indeed' London 45HLF8371+
1957 'Don't Knock The Rock', 'I Can't Find It' Brunswick+
1957 'Chu Chu Cha Boogie', 'Forty Cups Of Coffee' Brunswick 45-0-5658
1957 'Rockin' Rollin' Rover', '(You Hit The Wrong Note) Billy Goat' Brunswick 4 45-0-5688
1958 'Miss You', 'The Dipsy Doodle' Brunswick 45-0-5719
1958 'It's A Sin', 'Mary Mary Lou' Brunswick 45-0-5753
1958 'How Many?', 'Skinny Minny' Brunswick 45-0-5742
1958 'Don't Nobody Move', 'Lean Jean' Brunswick 45-0-5752
1959 'Chiquita Linda', 'Whoa Mabel' Brunswick 45-0-5766
1959 'Charmaine', 'I Got A Woman' Brunswick 45-0-5788
1959 'Caledonia', 'Shaky' Brunswick 45-0-5805
1959 'Joey's Song', 'Ooh Looka There Ain't She Pretty' Brunswick 45-0-5810
1960 'Puerto Rican Peddler', 'Smokiaan' Brunswick 45-0-5818
1960 'Candy Kisses', 'Tamiami' Warner Bros. 45WB6

EPs

1955 'Shake Rattle And Roll', 'ABC Boogie', 'Happy Baby', 'Dim Dim The Lights' Brunswick 9129
1955 'Pat A Cake', 'Fractured', 'Stop Beating Round The Mulberry Bush', 'Dance With A Dolly' London 1031
1956 'Razzle Dazzle', 'Two Hound Dogs', 'Burn That Candle', 'Rock A Beatin' Boogie' Brunswick 9214
1956 Rock Around The Clock', 'Mambo Rock', 'R-o-c-k', 'See You Later Alligator' Brunswick 9250
1956 'Live It Up', 'Real Rock Drive', 'Ten Little Indians', 'Chattanooga Choo-Choo London 1049
1956 'Rock The Joint', 'Rockin' Chair On The Moon', 'I'll Be True', 'Farewell So Long Goodbye' London 1050
1956 'Green Tree Boogie', 'Sundown Boogie', 'Juke Box Cannonball', 'Icy Heart' London 1058
1957 'Calling All the Comets', 'Rockin' Through The Rye', 'Hook Line And Sinker', 'Rudy's Rock' Brunswick 9278
1957 'A Rockin' Little Tune', 'Hide And Seek', 'Choo Choo Ch-Boogie', 'Blue Comet Blues' Brunswick 9279
1957 'Hey Then There Now', 'Goofin' Around', 'Hot Dog Buddy Buddy', 'Tonight's the Night' Brunswick 9280
1957 'See You Later Alligator', 'R-o-c-k', 'The Saints Rock And Roll', 'Burn That Candle' Brunswick LAT 8201

1957 'Dipsy Doodle', 'Miss You', 'Is It True What They Say About Dixie?', 'Carolina in The Morning' Brunswick 9349

1958 'You Can't Stop Me From Dreaming', 'I'll Be With You In Apple Blossom Time', 'Moon Over Miami', 'Please Don't Talk About Me' Brunswick 9350

1958 'Ain't Misbehavin'', 'One Sweet Letter From You', 'I'm Gonna Sit Right Down', 'Somebody Else Is Takin' My Place' Brunswick 9351

1959 'Pretty Alouette', 'Wooden Shoe Rock', 'Me Rock A Hula', 'Rockin' Rita' Brunswick 9446

1959 'A Fool Such As I', 'Where Did You Go Last Night', 'Sway With Me', 'Don't Nobody Move' Brunswick 9459

LPs

1956 'Live It Up', 'Real Rock Drive', 'Ten Little Indians', 'Chattanooga Choo Choo', 'Rock The Joint', 'Rockin' Chair On The Moon', 'I'll Be True', 'Farewell So Long Goodbye' London H-APB 1042

1956 'Rock Around The Clock', 'Shake Rattle And Roll', 'ABC Boogie', 'Thirteen Women', 'Razzle Dazzle', 'Two Hound Dogs', 'Dim Dim TheLights', 'Happy Baby', 'Birth Of The Boogie', 'Mambo Rock', 'Burn That Candle', 'Rock A Beatin' Boogie' Brunswick CAT 8117

1957 'Callin' All Comets', 'Rockin' Through The Rye', 'A Rockin' Little Tune', 'Hide And Seek',

Ronnie Hawkins in the late 1960's

'Hey Then There Now', 'Goofin' Around', 'Hook Line And Sinker', 'Rudy's Rock', 'Choo Choo Ch-Boogie', 'Blue Comet Blues', 'Hot Dog Buddy Buddy', 'Tonights The Night' Brunswick LAT 8139

1958 'Rockin' The Oldies': 'The Dipsy Doodle', 'You Can't Stop Me From Dreaming', 'I'll Be With You In Apple Blossom Time', 'Moon Over Miami', 'Is It True What They Say About Dixie?', 'Carolina In The Morning', 'Miss You', 'Please Don't Talk About Me When I'm Gone', 'Ain't Misbehavin ', 'One Sweet Letter From You', 'I'm Gonna Sit Right Down And Write Myself A Letter', 'Somebody Else Is Takin' My Place' Brunswick LAT 8219

1958 'Rockin' The Joint': 'New Rock The Joint', 'Move It On Over', 'How Many', 'See You Later Alligator', 'The Beak Speaks', 'Forty Cups Of Coffee', 'The Saints Rock And Roll', 'Sway With Me', 'It's A Sin', 'Burn That Candle' 'Rock Lomond', 'Rip It Up' Brunswick LAT 8268

1958 'Shake Rattle And Roll' on compilation album 'Let's Have A Party' Brunswick LAT 8271

1959 'Bill Haley's Chicks': 'Whoa Mabel', 'Ida Sweet As Apple Cider', 'Eloise', 'Dinah', 'Skinny Minny', 'Mary Mary Lou', 'Sweet Sue', 'B.B. Betty', 'Charmaine', 'Corrine Corrina', 'Marie', 'Lean Jean' Brunswick LAT 8295

1960 'Strictly Instrumental': 'Joey's Song', 'Music Music Music', 'Threepenny Opera Theme', 'In A Little Spanish Town', 'Two Shadows', 'Shaky', 'Seller', 'Smokiaan', 'Puerto Rican Peddler', 'Drowsy Wakers', 'Chiquita Linda', 'The Cat Walk' Brunswick LAT 8326

RONNIE HAWKINS

Like so many of the greatest white rock'n'rollers, Ronnie Hawkins is from the Southern states of America. He was born in 1937 in Huntsville, Arkansas, and lived there for the first twenty years of his life, soaking up the blues, gospel, country and hillbilly music which abounded in the south. He says he made his first record at the age of 16 'for one of those little fly-by-night companies; I cut a country tune, 'I Really Don't Want To Know', and 'Bo Diddley'. If this is true, he must have recorded 'Bo Diddley' before Bo Diddley himself, did but as the two men are supposed to have worked together for a while as cotton-pickers before Bo moved to Chicago, it is reasonable to suppose that Ronnie had already learnt the song in 1952.

Early in 1958, after a stint of army service and an abortive period at the University of Arkansas as a P.E. student, Ronnie formed a small group, playing C&W and blues around small-town clubs for just a handful of dollars a gig. The group consisted of Jimmy Ray Paulman on guitar, Willard 'Pop' Jones on piano, James Evans on bass guitar, and Levon Helm on drums. The going was tough, and the band did not need much persuading when Ronnie got a call from his old friend Conway Twitty, who was still a year away from hitting the big-time himself with 'Only Make Believe', suggesting they go to Canada, where there was some fairly well-paid club work available.

For a couple of years, Ronnie worked steadily in Canada, finding himself successful largely because his brand of deep south blues and rockabilly was something fresh and exciting to Canadian ears. 'I brought the first blues here' he says, 'nobody had ever heard of Bo Diddley, Muddy Waters, B.B. King or anyone in Canada'. He and the group, now christened 'The Hawks', did commute regularly back to the Northern U.S.A., however, and particularly to New York, because they had been signed to a recording contract with Roulette. Most of the material they cut was their versions of other peoples' rock'n'roll hits: 'Dizzy Miss Lizzy', 'Bo Diddley', 'Red Hot', etc. but they also did some of Ronnie's own compositions like 'Odessa' and 'Mary Lou'. Two of the singles released at this time made the Top 100 in the States: 'Forty Days', a slightly re-titled version of Chuck Berry's 'Thirty

Days', reached No. 45 in July 1959, and 'Mary Lou' climbed to No. 26 in the autumn of the same year, spending nearly four months in the chart.

From 1960 onwards, Ronnie based himself almost permanently in Canada, returning to the U.S.A. only to record for Roulette. The line-up of the Hawks also changed considerably over the next two or three years: Levon Helm stayed on, but a teenager named Robbie Robertson took over on lead guitar, and in came Richard Manuel on piano, ex-apprentice butcher Rick Danko on bass, and finally Garth Hudson, whom Ronnie considered 'a musical genius'. This was the group that was to play with Ronnie for some three years all over Canada, back him on some of his best discs, such as 'Who Do You Love' in 1963, and finally leave to seek separate fame as Levon And The Hawks, team up with Bob Dylan and become superstars of the

1970's as The Band. Ronnie's career didn't suffer much when he and the Hawks parted. He was known nationally in Canada, if virtually forgotten in the States by the mid-60's, and made plenty of money from slub and stage appearances, records [when his Roulette contract expired he started his own Hawk label in Canada] and clubs which he owned. To quote Kris Kristofferson, 'he has the instinct of a born horse-trader'. He did not return to the international limelight again until 1970, however, when he received sudden promotion from Rolling Stone magazine and John Lennon, and signed a recording contract with Atlantic. Since then, he has recorded prolifically again, most recently on Monument, and made a world tour for John Lennon's peace promotion effort. He rocks on in person and on record with as much drive and vitality as ever.

BRITISH RELEASES TO 1960

Singles

1959 'Thirty Days To Come Back', 'One Of These Days' Columbia 45DB4319

1959 'Mary Lou', 'Need Your Lovin' (Oh So Bad)' Columbia 45DB4345

1959 'Love Me Like You Can', 'Southern Love (What-Cha-Gonna-Do)' Columbia 45DB4412

1960 'Clara', 'Lonely Hours' Columbia 45DB4442

EPs

1960 'Rockin' With Ronnie': 'Odessa', 'My Gal Is Red Hot', 'Wild Little Willy', 'Ruby Baby' Columbia 7792

1960 'Rockin' With Ronnie No.

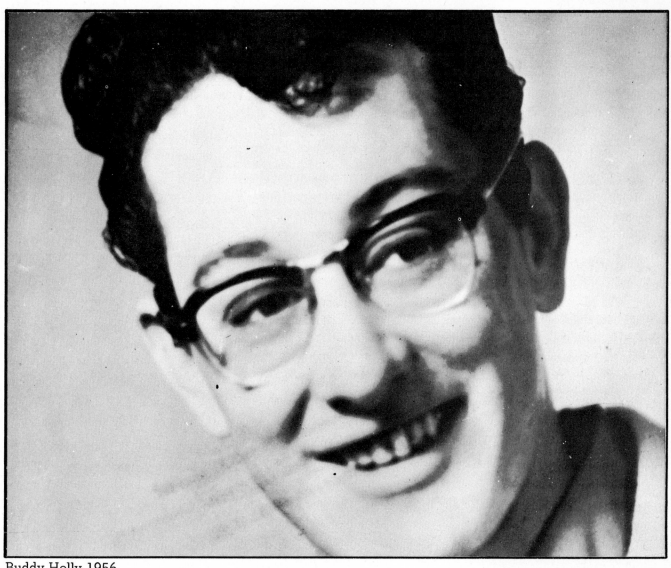

Buddy Holly 1956

2': 'What-Cha-Gonna-Do', 'Dizzy Miss Lizzy', 'Oh Sugar', 'Horace' Columbia 7795

LPs

1960 'Mr. Dynamo': 'Clara', 'Hey Boba Lou', 'Someone Like You', 'Dreams Do Come True', 'Hayride', 'Honey Don't', 'Lonely Hours', 'Sick And Tired', 'Love Me Like You Can', 'You Cheated You Lied', 'Baby Jean', 'Southern Love' Columbia 33SX 1238

1960 'Folk Ballads Of Ronnie Hawkins': 'Summertime', 'Sometimes', 'Feel Like A Mothers Child', 'I Gave My Love A Cherry', 'Brave Man', 'A Poor Wayfaring Stranger', 'Virginia Bride', 'Mister And Mississippi', 'John Henry', 'Fare Thee Well', 'Out Of A Hundred (The Death Of Floyd Collins)', 'Love From Afar' Columbia 33SX 1295

BEST RE-ISSUE AROUND

It's very hard to find re-issues of Ronnie's fifties material but in 1972 he released an excellent album called 'Rock And Roll Resurrection'. All but one track are fifties rock numbers, played in the spirit of the fifties, and with some excellent musicians in the backing band, including Boots Randolph on sax. Monument MNT 65122.

Tracks are: 'Lawdy Miss Clawdy', 'When My Dreamboat Comes Home', 'Cora Mae', 'Memphis Tennassee', 'Ain't That A Shame', 'Bony Moronie', 'Diddley Daddy', 'I'm In Love Again', 'Maybelline', 'The Same Old Song'

BUDDY HOLLY

Even at his raunchiest Buddy Holly was a much prettier performer than most of his contemporaries. His records from the important 1957/8 period were undoubtedly rock and roll but the vocal and instrumental feel was altogether lighter and less primitive sounding than most. And while he could cause a riot along with the wildest of them, like at the British concert in Nottingham, the riots usually involved dancing in the aisles rather than seat-slashing. But nevertheless he still stands today as one of the greatest rock and roll artists of the fifties: for the timeless quality of his songs rather than his image or impact on society. He also inspired a whole stream of second generation pop singers with his peculiar 'hiccuping' vocal style.

Born on 7th September 1936 in Lubbock, Texas, he was christened Charles Hardin Holley. In the early 1950's he started singing country and western material with a friend called Bob Montgomery, and the two had a regular Sunday radio show on KDAV coming out of Lubbock. They also made about a dozen recordings at Nesman Studios in Wichita Falls, a small town a few hundred miles from Lubbock. Most of the songs were written by Montgomery and are pretty uninspired country and western ditties. Many of these tracks are available today on the MCA LP 'Wishin'', MUPS 320.

Holly's break came in 1955 when he and Bob appeared on the same concert as Elvis in Lubbock. After the show a Decca talent scout called Jim Denny approached Holly and as a result he was signed to a one year contract with Decca. He made 16 tracks at Decca's Nashville studios, and though these were more rock oriented than the earlier Nesman cuts they were not particularly strong and little came of them. The band that backed Holly on the recordings was called the 'Three Tunes', and consisted of Jerry Allison on drums, later a member of the Crickets, Sonny Curtis on guitar and Don Guess on bass. Most of these tracks are now available on 'That'll Be The Day', Coral CP24.

So despite a considerable amount of recording work and significant local popularity, Holly was still on the bottom rungs of the music biz ladder when he met Norman Petty in 1956. Petty was a pianist and also the operator of a recording studio in Clovis, New Mexico. He became Buddy's manager, co-songwriter and confidant and guided his career almost until his death. He negotiated two recording contracts for Buddy: one as a solo artist with Coral and another as a member of the Crickets for Brunswick. The Crickets at this time were Jerry Allison, Niki Sullivan on guitar, Joe Maldin on bass, and of course Buddy.

During 1957 and 1958 some two dozen tracks were cut at Clovis, about half with the Crickets and about half 'solo', although the Crickets often provided the backing on these tracks too. This was the most productive and inspired period in Holly's career and many of the cuts were hits during his lifetime. Perhaps the best ones were 'Oh Boy', 'Not Fade Away', 'Maybe Baby', 'It's Too Late', and 'That'll Be The Day', all with the Crickets; and 'Peggy Sue', 'Rave On', 'Listen To Me', 'Words Of Love', 'Everyday', 'Heartbeat', all solo. In very general terms the tracks with the Crickets tend to be the raunchiest. Most of the Crickets tracks are available today on the Coral LP 'Chirpin' Crickets', CP 20, and most of the better solo ones on 'Listen To Me', MCA MUPS 5312.

In 1958 Buddy married a Puerto Rican girl called Maria Elena Santiago and the two moved to an apartment in New York. The Crickets didn't move north with them though, and the recordings made in this period were either made at home by Buddy on his own tape recorder or in the studio with largish orchestras.

Buddy and the Crickets appeared together still on live gigs though and it was after one of these concerts at the Surf Ballroom in Iowa that he was involved in the plane crash that killed him, on February 3rd 1959.

After his death, Petty continued to release material Buddy had recorded during his lifetime, mostly with newly recorded backing tracks dubbed on. He had big posthumous hits with 'Peggy Sue Got Married' in 1959; 'Baby I Don't Care' in 1961; 'Reminiscing' in 1962; 'Brown Eyed Handsome Man' in 1963; 'Bo Diddley' in 1963; 'Wishing' in 1963. The Crickets continued as a performing and recording group until 1965.

Magazine articles abound on Holly in the music press today but the most comprehensive account of his life and music is Dave Laing's book 'Buddy Holly', Studio Vista. The book also contains a very full discography of all Holly's issued and unissued recordings and is worth buying for this alone.

BRITISH RELEASES TO 1960
+British Top 20 Hit
Singles

1957 'Blue Days Black Nights', 'Love Me' Brunswick 45-0-5581

1957**I'm Looking For Someone To Love', 'That'll Be The Day, Vogue Coral45Q72279+

1958 'Every Day', 'Peggy Sue' Vogue Coral 45Q72293+

1958**'Not Fade Away', 'Oh Boy' Vogue Coral 45Q72298+

1958 'I'm Gonna Love You Too', 'Listen To Me' Vogue Coral 45Q72288+

1958 'Rave On', 'Take Your Time' Vogue Coral 45Q72325+

1958 'Early In The Morning', 'Now We're One' Vogue Coral 45Q72333+

1958**'Maybe Baby', 'Tell Me How' Vogue Coral 45Q72307+

1958**'It's So Easy', 'Lonesome Tears' Vogue Coral 45Q72343

1958**'Fools Paradise', 'Think It Over' Vogue Coral 45Q72329+

1959 'Heartbeat', 'Well Alright' Vogue Coral 45Q72346

1959 'It Doesn't Matter Any More', 'Raining In My Heart' Vogue Coral 45Q72360+

1959 'Midnight Shift', 'Rock Around With Ollie Vee' Brunswick 45-0-5800

1959 'Cryin' Waitin' Hopin ', 'Peggy Sue' Vogue Coral 45Q72376+

1959**'Loves Made A Fool Of You', 'Someone Someone' Vogue Coral 45Q72365

1960 'Every Day', 'Heartbeat' Vogue Coral 45Q72393

EPs

1958 'Listen To Me', 'Peggy Sue', 'I'm Gonna Love You Too', 'Every Day' Coral 2002

1959 'Rave On': 'Rave On', 'Take Your Time', 'Early In The Morning', 'Now We're One' Coral 2005

1959 'Heartbeat': 'Heartbeat', 'Well Alright', 'You're So Square', 'Little Baby' Coral 2015

1958**'Oh Boy', 'Not Fade Away', 'Maybe Baby', 'Tell Me How' Coral 2003

1959**'It's So Easy': 'It's So Easy', 'Lonesome Tears', 'Think It Over', 'Fools Paradise' Coral 2014

1959 'It Doesn't Matter Any More', 'Heartbeat', 'Rainin' In My Heart', 'Early In The Morning' Coral 2032

1959 'You Are My One Desire', 'Blue Days Black Nights', 'Modern Don Juan' 'Ting A Ling' Brunswick 9456

1960 'Girl On My Mind', 'Love Me', 'I'm Changing All Those Changes', 'Don't Come Knockin' Brunswick 9457

1960 'The Late Great Buddy Holly': 'Look At Me', 'Ready Teddy', 'Mailman Bring Me No More Blues', 'Words Of Love' Coral 2044

1960 'Raining In My Heart' on compilation EP 'Hitsville Vol. 1' Coral 2034

LPs

1958 'I'm Gonna Love You Too', 'Peggy Sue', 'Look At Me', 'Listen To Me', 'Valley Of Tears', 'Ready Teddy', 'Every Day', 'Mailman Bring Me No More Blues', 'Words Of Love', 'Baby I Don't Care', 'Little Baby' Coral CVA 9085

1959**'Chirpin' Crickets': 'Oh Boy', 'Not Fade Away', 'You've Got To Love Me', 'Maybe Baby', 'It's Too Late', 'Tell Me How', 'That'll Be The Day', 'I'm Looking For Someone To Love', 'An Empty Cup', 'Send Me Some Love', 'Last Night', 'Rock Me My Baby' Coral LVA 9081

1960 'The Buddy Holly Story': 'Raining In My Heart', 'Early In The Morning', 'Peggy Sue', 'Maybe Baby', 'Every Day', 'Rave On', 'That'll Be The Day', 'Heartbeat', 'Think It Over', 'Oh Boy', 'It's So Easy', 'It Doesn't Matter Any More'. Coral LVA 9105 'That'll Be The Day', 'Oh Boy', 'Maybe Baby', 'It's So Easy', 'Think It Over', are with the Crickets.

1961 'Buddy Holly Story Vol.2': 'Peggy Sue', 'Well Alright', 'What To Do', 'That Makes It Tough', 'Now We're One', 'Take Your Time', 'Crying Waiting Hoping', 'True Love Ways', 'Learning the Game', 'Little Baby', 'Moondreams', 'That's What They Say' Coral CVA 9127

** Denotes record made with the Crickets.

JOHNNY AND THE HURRICANES

Johnny and the Hurricanes were among the few groups who managed to find consistent commercial success with purely instrumental records during the late 50's and early 60's. Even by the standards of playing which were expected in those days, they were a fairly average bunch of musicians, but they had two distinctive trademarks: Firstly, they used the innovation of a Hammond organ as the lead melody instrument on their discs, instead of guitar or saxophone as was usually done. Second, their singles material, in the early days at least, was exceptionally well-chosen, being rocked-up versions of old folk tunes on which the original melody line was still easily recognisable. Both these factors played a large part in their success.

The group was five-strong, with the original personnel being Johnny Paris, sax, Paul Tesluk, organ, Dave York, guitar, Butch Mattice, bass, and Lynn Bruce, drums. In 1960, Bruce was replaced by Bill 'Bo' Savitch. They met while at high school in Toledo, Ohio, and started to play semi-professionally at high school dances, etc., before securing a residency in Toledo's Pearson Park entertainment centre during the summer of 1958. This brought them regional acclaim, some club bookings, and a few local TV air shots, plus a recording contract with Warwick Records.

The group's first Warwick release was a pounder called 'Crossfire', which strongly featured leader/saxophonist Johnny Paris. Released in the spring of 1959, it was an almost immediate hit and only just failed to enter the U.S. top 20, spending a healthy three months in the mid-regions of the charts. For the follow-up, they found an old cowboy song called 'Red River Valley', arranged it for the elctric organ, with sax and guitar breaks over a solid beat, and retitled it 'Red River Rock'. The record was a blockbuster. It soared to No. 5 in the U.S.A. during September 1959, and two months later peaked at No. 2 on this side of the Atlantic. It is said to have sold

(left to right: back row Paul Tesluck, Dave York, Butch Mattice, Lynn Bruce; foreground: Johnny Paris)

Buddy Knox (centre) with Jimmy Bowen (left) and Donnie Lanier in Disk Jockey Jamboree.

over three million copies, and to this day is the tune for which the group are mostly remembered.

More hits followed during 1960. There was 'Reveille Rock', a beat version of the old bugle call, then 'Beatnik Fly', from 'Blue Tail Fly', 'Down Yonder', and 'Rockin' Goose'. At this point, American sales bagan to tail off, although in Britain the group could do no wrong, as the No. 2 chart placing of 'Rockin' Goose' testified: in the U.S.A. it only reached No. 60. Another string of 'oldies' followed, in an obvious attempt to recapture the 'Red River Rock' hit feel. it didn't really work, however, as 'You Are My Sunshine' and 'Ja Da' met with progressively decreasing success, and the group fell from grace in Britain too, bowing out with 'High Voltage', 'Old Smokie', their chart swan-song in mid-1961.

The group did not break up after they ceased making hits. In fact, they did not make their first visit to Britain until early in 1963, where they were well- received by audiences which had stopped buying their discs in favour of instrumentals by, amongst others, the Tornados, whose main claim to fame was that they had borrowed the Hurricanes' lead organ sound on the 'Telstar' million-seller.

Instrumental records by Johnny & The Hurricanes continued to be issued by two or three hopeful labels in succession, but they changed to vocals as the 1960's wore on. And as recently as 1971, the group could be heard playing in Germany, under a different name, and they are now apparently well into the rock'n'roll revival bag.

BRITISH RELEASES TO 1960
+British Top 20 Hit

Singles

1959 'Crossfire', 'Lazy' London 45HL8899

1959 'Buckeye', 'Red River Rock' London 45HL8948+

1959 'Reveille Rock', 'Time Bomb' London 45HL9017+

1960 'Beatnik Fly', 'Sandstorm' London 45HL19072+

1960 Down Yonder', 'Sheba' London 45HLX9134+

1960 'Rocking Goose', 'Revival' London 45HLX9190+

BUDDY KNOX

Buddy was born on 14th April 1933, in Happy, Texas. He learned guitar while at high school, and then moved on to the West Texas State College to study psychology and business administration. Here he met Jimmy Bowen, Don Lanier and Dave Alldred, and the four formed a group called the Rhythm Orchids which played college dates and other local bookings.

Buddy and Jimmy Bowen wrote a couple of original numbers for the group, 'Party Doll' and 'I'm Sticking With You', which proved so popular that they decided to have a stab at recording both. The Rhythm Orchids trekked to Norman Petty's studio in nearby Clovis, New Mexico, and a disc was cut, with Buddy singing 'Party Doll' and Jimmy vocalising on 'I'm Stickin' With You'. Lacking a recording contract as such, they formed a label of their own called Triple-D, and got the record distributed around the immediate north-west Texas area. It sold well, paying off nicely in extra bookings, but also bringing a problem to the group: straight out of college, they did not have the financial resources between them to give Triple-D any national promotion or distribution. For the record to be a real hit, it would have to be sold to a national label, which it was, late in 1956, to the newly-formed Roulette concern in New York.

Roulette, not only bought the Triple-D masters, but also gave recording contracts to Knox and Bowen as featured soloists. 'I'm Stickin' With You' and 'Party Doll' were re-issued separately, billed as by Jimmy Bowen and Buddy Knox respectively, with two more songs by Jimmy on the B-sides, although 'My Baby's Gone,' on the flip of 'Party Doll' was credited on the label to Buddy. Both discs entered the charts simultaneously in February 1957; 'Stickin'' climbed to No. 14, but 'Party Doll' went on to top the charts, sell over a million copies, and spend upwards of five months on the Top 100.

In a sudden whirl of T.V. appearances and one-night-stand package tours, Buddy was a rock'n'roll star. He followed up 'Party Doll' in similar style with 'Rock Your Little Baby To Sleep', which only climbed to 23, but spent 16 weeks in the charts. Then came the bouncy Hawiian-flavoured 'Hula Love', which

reached No. 12 and had another five-month chart residency. For fourteen solid months, from February 1957 to April 1958, Buddy had discs in the U.S. Top 100 without a week's break.

1958 saw a slight drop in sales, although simultaneously Buddy was drafted into the army, and did a stint of several months in the Tank Corps. He filmed a spot in 'Disc Jockey Jamboree', alongside Jerry Lee Lewis and others, whilst on weekend leave, and this helped to keep him in the public eye whilst hits like 'Swingin' Daddy', 'Somebody Touched Me', 'That's Why I Cry', 'Teasable, Pleasable You' and 'I Think I'm gonna Kill Myself' followed each other into the middle regions of the Top 100.

Once out of the army, Buddy resumed touring, appearing in several of Alan Freed's coast-to-coast treks along with a host of other rock stars. His last couple of discs for Roulette, however, failed to register, and his

contract was not renewed when it expired in 1960. He signed with Liberty in Hollywood, and made the charts again with his first disc for the label, 'Lovey Dovey', towards the end of the year. It reached No. 25, but turned out to be a short-lived revival of fortune, since the follow-up, 'Ling Ting Tong', which reached No. 65 in April 1961, proved to be his swan-song on the American charts. His only later taste of success was with 'She's Gone', which made the British Top 50 in the summer of 1962.

Throughout the rest of the 1960's, Buddy continued to record prolifically on a variety of labels, such as Ruff, Reprise, and latterly United Artists, but failed to find much in the way of commercial success. Regular club appearances, however, provided steady work, and the recording of some more country-slanted material broadened his appeal. In the early 1970's he visited Britain.

BRITISH RELEASES TO 1960
Singles
1957 'My Baby's Gone', 'Party Doll' Parlophone R3914
1957 'Devil Woman', 'Hula Love' Columbia 45DB4014
1957 'Swingin' Daddy', 'Whenever I'm Lonely' Columbia 45DB4077
1958 'C'mon Baby', 'Somebody Touched Me', Columbia 45DB4180
1959 'I Think I'm Gonna Kill Myself', 'To Be With You' Columbia 45DB4302
1960 'I Got You', 'Lovey Dovey' London 45HLG9268
EPs
1958 'Rock-A-Buddy Knox': 'Mary Lou', 'Rockhouse', 'Maybelline', 'Devil Woman' Columbia 45EP7732

JERRY LEE LEWIS

'The Killer' was born in the small town of Ferriday, Louisiana, on 29th September 1935. Both his parents sang and played at the Assembly Of God church, and his father played guitar at home. Louisiana contains a wide variety of musical forms, from country music to swamp blues, and as he grew up Jerry Lee became exposed to all of them. And it's reflected in his music today; he seems equally at home with rock and roll, country or straight pop.

His parents mortgaged their small home in order to buy a piano for Jerry, and soon music became the main interest in his life. The first time he played in public was in the Ford Agency in Ferriday. The local dealer was introducing his new line while a country and western band was playing in the car lot. Jerry joined in for about twenty minutes, singing and playing on 'Drinkin' Wine Spoo Dee O Dee'. He was just thirteen. During this period Jerry spent much of his free time hanging out at Haney's Big House, a local dance hall presenting blues bands, and it was here that he was first deeply exposed to black music.

At 14 he got his first night club job at the Blue Cat Club in Natchez. But the pace of going to school by day and playing at night was too much for him and he had to leave the job. But he continued playing local clubs at weekends, first the Hilltop and later the Wagon Wheel. Paul Whitehead, a blind piano player, was the leader of the band at the Wheel, and Jerry mainly played drums.

In his final year at High School, Jerry already had a sizeable local following and was set on a career in music. Hank Williams, Elvis and Bing Crosby were his favourites and his material ranged from swing standards like 'Stardust', to country numbers like 'Cheatin' Heart', taking in boogie and blues on the way. This plurality of taste has remained with him. Almost alone among the major fifties rock performers, Jerry Lee did not write his own material: it wasn't songs he sold so much as high power performances.

In February 1956, he drove the 300 miles to Memphis to try and get an audition with Sam Phillips of Sun Records. Phillips was in Miami at the time but Jack Clements, a member of the Sun staff made some tapes of Jerry; he also told him that Sun thought Elvis had so completely dominated the rock and roll market that that type of music was drying up saleswise!

A month went by and Jerry had heard nothing from Sun, so he returned to Memphis to try and see Phillips again. Clements saw him and said 'We think the record has something'. Phillips had listened to the tapes on his return from Miami and liked what he heard.

Sun's first Jerry Lee release was Ray Price's Country hit 'Crazy Arms'. It did well in the country field but didn't figure in the rock and roll/pop charts. But it did stimulate greater Southern interest in Jerry and soon he was doing gigs in the neighbouring States for the first time. His booker at the time was the ex-Memphis DJ Bob Neal, who was also booking Gene Vincent.

The second record was the big breakthrough: 'Whole Lotta Shakin' Goin' On', 1957. A volcanic rocker, which Jerry had been performing live for four years. It was No. 1 in the country, Pop and R&B charts simultaneously, a unique occurence in American popular music. An appearance on the Steve Allen show really broke Jerry wide upen and he started doing concerts all over the U.S. for promoter Oscar Brown.

'Great Balls Of Fire', also 1957, established Jerry as a major star, a position he continued to hold until about 1960/1 having big hits with 'Breathless', 1958, 'High School Confidential', 1959, 'Loving Up A Storm', 1959, and 'What'd I Say', 1961.

Despite 'Breathless', 1958 was a dodgy year for Jerry Lee. He came over for a British tour with his second wife, and it was found that she was only 13 years old. The press butchered him and he had to cancel most of the tour, after being booed off stage during his first show.

The 'B' sides of the records even in the rock and roll period were generally country numbers and from 1968 this is the style he has developed in recording work. In 1968 the country 'Another Place Another Time' became his biggest chart success since 1962.

1968 was also memorable for Jerry for the part he had in 'Catch My Soul', the rock version of Othello which ran for six weeks at the Ahmanson Theatre in Los Angeles.

Jerry Lee still does well over 200 dates a year, with frequent visits to Europe. He has just completed an album here in London called the 'London Sessions' on Mercury: good rocking stuff if a little over-extended in production.

Jerry Lee Lewis in Disk Jockey Jamboree

You shake my nerves and you
rattle my brain
Too much love drives a man   Mar 58
insane
You broke my wheel but what a
thrill   Apr 58
Goodness gracious great balls of
fire.
Great Balls Of Fire   Sep 58
(Hammer/Blackwell) Carlin Music.
BRITISH RELEASES TO 1960
+British Top 20 Hit
    Singles
Aug 57 'It'll Be Me', 'Whole
    Lotta Shakin' Goin' On'
    London 45HLS8457+
Jan 58 'Great Balls Of Fire',

'Mean Woman Blues'
London 45HLS8529+
'I'm Feeling Sorry',
'You Win Again'
London 45HLS8559
'Breathless' 'Down The
Line' London
45HLS8592+
'Break Up', 'I'll Make It
All Up To You' London
45HLS 8700
Jan 59 'Fools Like Me','High
    School Confidential'
    London 45HLS8780+
May 59 'Big Blon' Baby',
    'Lovin' Up A Storm'
    London 45HLS8840+

Sep 59 ' Let's Talk About Us',
    'The Ballad Of Lil' Joe'
    London 45HLS8941
Nov 59 'I Could Never Be
    Ashamed', 'Little
    Queenie' London
    45HLS8993
May 60 'Baby Baby Bye Bye',
    'Old Black Joe' London
    45HLS9131
Oct 60 'John Henry', 'Hang Up
    My Rock And Roll
    Shoes' London
    45HLS9202
Dec 60 'I'll Sail My Ship
    Alone', 'It Hurt Me So'
    London 45HLS9083

Carl Perkins on stage 1969

	EPs
1958	'It'll Be Me', 'Whole Lotta Shakin' Goin' On', 'Great Balls Of Fire', 'You Win Again' London 1140
1959	'Don't Be Cruel', 'Put Me Down', 'Who Will Buy The Wine', 'Crazy Arms' London 1186
1959	'No. 3': 'Jambalaya', 'Fools Like Me', 'High School Confidential',

'When The Saints Go Marchin' In' London 1187

	LPs
1959	'Don't Be Cruel', 'Goodnight Irene', 'Put Me Down', 'It All Depends', 'Ubangi Stomp', 'Crazy Arms', 'Jambalaya', 'Fools Like Me', 'High School Confidential', 'When The Saints Go Marchin'

In', 'Matchbox', 'It'll Be Me' London HA-S2138

There are many Jerry Lee re-issues around today, and for rock material the L.P. 'Original Golden Hits Vol. 1' is the best, containing all the early rock chart successes. Philips SBL7622.
Another excellent album is 'Live At The Star Club Hamburg'; backed by the very fine British band, the Nashville Teens.

CARL PERKINS

Carl was born on the 9th April, 1932, in Tipton County Tennessee. Interested in music from a very early age, he learned to play guitar as a child, and formed a family group with his two older brothers, Clayton and Jay. The music they played as amateurs through their teens and early twenties was basically Country & Western, although Carl favoured C&W 'with a beat', and admits to a strong black influence in his formative style. Listening to his compositions like 'Matchbox', the country blues influence is easy to hear.

In 1955, when they were playing professionally in the Memphis area, the Perkins brothers, Carl on vocals and lead, Jay on rhythm guitar and Clayton on stand- up bass, were spotted by Sam Phillips, owner or Sun records, and a man who also liked his country with a beat. Phillips was then in the process of signing up and recording most of the local talent who featured this Rockabilly style. He had already found Elvis Presley and scored tremendous success with this young white country boy who sang like a negro, so Carl & Co. seemed a good bet for similar things. Two singles were recorded and issued: 'Turn Around' and 'Let The Jukebox Keep On Playing', which were both Carl's own compositions. They did well enough to satisfy Phillips that he'd found something worthwhile, and got the Perkins brothers a spot on a tour of the south, along with Presley and another new Sam Phillips find, Johnny Cash.

Then, at the very end of 1955, came Carl's third disc and his greatest success. Another self-composition, the song has remained a rock classic to this day, has been sung or recorded by every artist who has been associated with R&B, and by its very perenniality has kept Carl's name to the fore in music ever since. 'Blue Suede Shoes', of course. It soared into the national charts early in 1956, and before leaving them twenty-one weeks later, reached No. 4 and sold over a million copies.

However, disaster struck almost immediately. On 23rd March, while they were travelling by car to guest in the Perry Como show, the brothers were involved in a fatal smash. Jay Perkins received injuries from which he later died, and Carl was put out of action for several months. He very nearly fell out of the public eye as quickly as he had entered it, being unable to promote his 'Shoes' follow-up 'Boppin' The Blues', which scraped to a mere No. 60 in the Top 100. A previously filmed appearance in the film 'Disc Jockey Jamboree' with a host of other rock stars, filled the void temporarily. Carl was seen singing 'Glad All Over', for once not one of his own songs. However, in those halcyon days, new rock stars were appearing in droves almost overnight, and Carl just couldn't manage the comeback. He rejoined the also-rans.

In 1958, when his Sun contract expired, Carl was signed by Columbia. They had missed the boat almost completely in the early days of rock, and much belatedly were gathering up erstwhile R&B hitmakers in order to repromote them; they acquired Johnny Cash at the same time. Carl worked and recorded steadily, but apart from a minor hit in 1959 with 'Pointed Toe Shoes', stayed strictly small-time. It was not until 1963-4, by which time he'd moved on again to U.S. Decca, that he found renewed public interest, or at least his compositions did: 'Honey Don't', 'Matchbox' and 'Everybody's Trying To Be My Baby' were recorded by the Beatles, who announced that Carl had been one of the rock greats, and their listening public took note and began to enquire after him again. He came to England in 1964, performed and even recorded here.

British and European success, however, did not necessarily mean a revival of fortunes in the States, and America in 1964/5 was in the throes of the British Invasion, and hardly wanted to know its own talent, least of all a forgotten rock'n'roller. Carl went into virtual retirement from the music world, and took to farming.

In 1967, while still virtually inactive as a performer but having sorted out his personal problems, Carl made some records for the Dollie Label, which featured him purely in a modern Country vein. One of his old labels, Columbia, became interested again and re-signed him, and Carl returned to public appearances as part of Johnny Cash's touring group. He has remained with Cash ever since, playing both as a backing musician and as a soloist, and featuring both C&W material and his old rock classics. Columbia recorded him in a rock/R&B vein at first, including an album of remakes of his hits and one which teamed him with the rock revival group NRBQ. However, over the last three years he has veered once again towards C&W on disc, and

The Platters at a London press reception preceding their 1957 British tour.

songs like 'Cotton Top' have been putting him into the Country charts in the U.S.A.

BRITISH RELEASES TO 1960
+British Top 20 Hit
Singles

June 56 'Blue Suede Shoes', 'Honey Don't' London 45HLU8271+

May 57 'Matchbox', 'Your True Love' London 45HLS8408

Jan 58 'Forever Young', 'Glad All Over' London 45HLS8527

May 58 'Lend Me Your Comb', 'That's Right' London 45HLS8608

Aug 59 'I Don't See Me In Your Eyes Any More', 'One Ticket To Loneliness' Philips PB983

LPs

1959 'Blue Suede Shoes',

'Movie Mag', 'Sure To Fall In Love With You', 'Gone Gone Gone', 'Honey Don't, 'Only You', 'Tennessee', 'Wrong Yo Yo', 'Everybody's Tryin' To Be My Baby', 'Matchbox', 'Your True Love', 'Boppin' The Blues' London HAS2202

THE PLATTERS

The Platters were the vocal group of the 1950's, in terms of success on records. In an era when chart consistency was chiefly the prerogative of solo rock'n'roll artists, and most groups were one-shot hitmakers, the Platters acquired six gold records and upwards of two dozen chart entries.

Much of the credit for this tremendous run of success can be attributed to the group's manager, Buck Ram, who was also their producer, arranger and chief songwriter. Buck formed the group in 1953, with Tony Williams as lead tenor, and Alex Hodge, Herb Reed and David Lynch supporting him; none of them having had much professional music experience, but all having sung in church and gospel choirs and having done the rounds of local nightclub appearances to boost their daytime earnings from non-musical jobs. The group was signed to King records of Cincinnati, and had several singles released on King's subsidiary, Federal, selling reasonably well within the specialist R&B market.

Ram however, wanted bigger things for the Platters. To augment the sound, he brought in girl vocalist Zola Taylor from the Queens, and also Paul Roci as baritone voice, to replace Alex Hodge who had decided to leave. The group also got a new recording contract, in a rather roundabout way: Mercury records, one of the biggest labels in the country, made an offer for the Penguins, who were also managed by Buck Ram, and had just had a million-seller with 'Earth Angel'. Buck agreed to let the Penguins sign, but only on the condition that Mercury took the Platters as well. The label chiefs must have cursed him at the time as a sharp operator, but they agreed, and in doing so signed themselves into one of their best-ever deals. The Penguins never made the charts again, but the Platters erupted.

The group's first Mercury release was a Ram composition which they had recorded previously for Federal, 'Only You'. Buck brought in a new arrangement for the number which emphasised Tony Williams' soaring tenor voice, and immediately the record was a success. It leapt into the American charts in the late autumn of 1955 and went to No. 5, selling over a million copies by the end of the year. Whilst still high in the charts, it was joined by an even faster-rising hit in 'The Great Pretender', a dramatic Williams showcase which reached No. 1 at the end of January 1956. The Platters' greatest year had begun, and their discs could do no wrong.

No sooner had 'Pretender' collected its gold disc, than 'The Magic Touch' shot to No. 4 and went gold too. The flipside of this, 'Winner Take all', made the charts in its own right, and this was a trend which was to be repeated throughout the year by other Platter hits.

The fourth million-seller came along in 'My Prayer', a ballad which returned the group to the No. 1 spot for two weeks during August. The flipside, 'Heaven On Earth', reached No. 39. Then came 'You'll Never, Never Know', 'It Isn't Right' and 'One In A Million', 'On My Word Of Honour', both sides of both discs entering the Top 30 to complete a truly amazing year of hitmaking.

The group appeared in hugely successful rock package shows, made many T.V. appearances, and were also featured in Alan Freed's film 'Rock Around The Clock', which gave the British audience a chance to see them.

U.K. acceptance of the group came slightly later because 'Only You' was not issued here at the time of its American success, and the cover version by the Hilltoppers had it all its own way, reaching No. 3. In August, however, 'The Great Pretender' was issued with 'Only You' as the flipside, and the double-sided hit coupling climbed to No. 5, to be rapidly followed by 'My Prayer' which reached No. 4.

1957 brought no gold discs for the Platters, but continued the stream of hits with 'I'm Sorry', 'He's Mine', 'My Dream' and 'Only Because'. In 1958, however, they returned to the top slot, and No. 3 in Britain, with 'Twilight Time', another gold disc, bringing the total to five. 'You're Making A Mistake' and 'I Wish' rode the charts in a minor way, and then at the end of the year came perhaps the classic Tony Williams ballad performance, 'Smoke Gets In Your Eyes'. This was a U.S. and British No. 1 almost simultaneously at the beginning of 1959, and for once was not a Buck Ram song but an oldie written in 1933.

After the smash success of 'Smoke', the group's appeal started to dwindle slightly during the rest of 1959 and 1960, possibly because their style had not changed at all since 1955, and was beginning to sound dated to many record buyers. The biggest hits were 'Enchanted' which reached No. 12 in 1959, and 'To Each His Own' and 'Harbour Lights', attaining positions 21 and 8 respectively in 1960. The latter of these two also made No. 12 in Britain, and was their U.K. chart swansong.

In 1961, after a slight revival with 'If I Didn't Care' and 'I'll Never Smile Again', both of which made the U.S. top 30, Tony Williams left the group to go solo, obviously somewhat disillusioned, and of the opinion that his voice was becoming faulty and needed vocal training. Unfortunately, his few solo efforts on record met with no success, and he disappeared from the scene completely.

After Williams' departure, the group was left stranded without their main attraction. They continued to record with new lead singer Sonny Turner, but public interest had turned elsewhere, and after a very minor Top 100 touch with 'It's Magic' in 1962, the hits stopped coming. The group did not break up, but various of the 50's personnel began to drift away, including Zola Turner, who left in 1964. Eventually, their Mercury contract having expired in the mid-sixties, the Platters signed with Musicor, still shepherded by Buck Ram, and started virtually a new career as a soul goup, scoring a fair proportion of minor hits around 1966/7 with such discs as 'I'll Love You 1,000 Times' and 'Washed Ashore'. Today, somewhere on the U.S. soul scene, they are still performing.

BRITISH RELEASES TO 1960
+British Top 20 Hit
Singles
1955 'Beer Barrel Boogie', 'Roses Of Picardy' Parlophone DP506
1956 'Magic Touch', 'Winner Take All' Mercury MT107
1956 'Heaven On Earth', 'My Prayer' Mercury MT120+
1956 'It Isn't Right', 'You'll Never Never Know' Mercury MT130
1957 'On My Word Of Honour', 'One In A Million' Mercury MT143
1957 'I'm Sorry', 'He's Mine' Mercury MT145+
1957 'I Wanna', 'My Dream' Mercury MT156
1957 'Helpless', 'Indifferent' Mercury MT197
1958 'Are You Sincere', 'Don't Let Go' Mercury 7MT205
1958 'Out Of My Mind', 'Twilight Time' Mercury 7MT214+
1958 'My Old Flame', 'You're Making A Mistake' Mercury 7MT227
1958 'I Wish', 'It's Raining Outside' Mercury 45AMT1001
1959 'No Matter What You Are', 'Smoke Gets In Your Eyes' Mercury 45AMT1016+
'Enchanted', 'The Sound And The Fury' Mercury 45AMT1039
1959 'Love Of A Lifetime', 'Remember When' Mercury 45AMT1053
1959 'My Blue Heaven', 'Wish It Were Me' Mercury 45AMT1066
1959 'My Secret', 'What Does It Matter' Mercury 45AMT1076
1960 'Harbour Lights', 'By The Sleepy Lagoon' Mercury 45AMT1081+
1960 'Apple Blossom Time', 'Ebb Tide' Mercury 45AMT1098
1960 'Red Sails In The Sunset', 'Sad River' Mercury 45AMT1106
1960 'Down The River Of Golden dreams', 'To Each His Own' Mercury 45AMT1118
1960 'If I Didn't Dare', 'True Lover' Mercury 45AMT1128

The Platters 1957

49

ELVIS PRESLEY

Bill Haley may have been the first rock and roll star, but Elvis was the first <u>teenage</u> rock and roll star, and the biggest ever. He was born on 8th January, 1935 in Tupelo, Mississippi, but soon after moved to Memphis with his family. As a teenager he did pretty much what his parents told him to, and seemed to be happy to do so. At School he seems to have been almost invisible: today, no-one remembers much about him. He was always polite, calling older people ma'am or sir, he didn't drink, didn't smoke, didn't gamble and didn't smash up his cars. All admirable virtues but hardly fitting in with his stage presence or early vocal style.

In fact his stage persona in the fifties was probably a reaction against all this good behaviour, and Elvis at the time was probably into a sort of Jekyll and Hyde trip. Who is to say which Elvis was the real Elvis? Was it Colonel Parker's good boy or the hip wiggling, black voiced singer? But who cares anyway. He was a breath of fresh air to young record buyers and a breath of poison to middle America.

Then he went into the army, and came out tamed. True he has made some upbeat records since the fifties, but upbeat records on their own do not rock and roll make.

SOME ELVIS FIRSTS

First job : cinema usher in Memphis.

First recording : 'My Happiness' 1953. Elvis wanted to give his mother a special birthday present. He took time off from his truck driving job to do a two dollar record in a local studio, where he recorded his mother's favourite song. The owner of the studio was Sam Phillips of Sun Records, who later gave Elvis his first recording contract.

First record company : Sun Records. In 1954 Elvis was signed by Sam Phillips. The first record he made for Sun was 'That's Alright Mama'. On these early sessions Elvis was backed by Scotty Moore, guitar, and Bill Black, bass. These two were also to back him in concert during much of his pre-army career.

First radio appearance : on Memphis DJ Dewey Phillips radio show, 1954.

First T.V. commercial : for Southern Made Doughnuts, 1954.

First managers : Scotty Moore and Bob Neal.

First important stage show : with Slim Whitman in Memphis, July 1954.

First T.V. show appearance : Louisiana Hayride, March 1955.

First RCA recording : 'Heartbreak Hotel', 1956.

First film : 'Love Me Tender', 1956

First million seller : 'Heartbreak Hotel'.

First No. 1 in the U.S.A. : 'Heartbreak Hotel'.

First U.K. release : 'Heartbreak Hotel'.

First No. 1 in U.K. : 'All Shook Up', July 1957.

First journey outside the U.S.A. : to Germany with the army September 1958.

First visit to U.K. : Prestwick Airport, Scotland, March 1960. Changing aircraft on the way back to the States from Germany, where he had been with the army.

BRITISH RELEASES TO 1960
+British Top 20 Hit

Singles

1956	'Heartbreak Hotel', 'I Was The One' HMV7M385+
1956	'Blue Suede Shoes', 'Tutti Frutti' HMV7M405+
1956	'I Forgot To Remember To Forget', 'Mystery Train' HMV7MC42
1956	'I Want You I Need You I Love You', 'My Baby Left Me' HMV7M424+
1956	'Don't Be Cruel', 'Hound Dog' HMV45POP249+
1956	'Blue Moon', 'I Don't Care If The Sun Don't Shine' HMV45POP272+
1956	'Anyway You Want Me', 'Love Me Tender' HMV45POP253+
1957	'Love Me', 'Mystery Train' HMV45POP295
1957	'Baby Lets Play House', 'Rip It Up' HMV45POP305
1957	'Playin' For Keeps', 'Too Much' HMV45POP330+
1957	'All Shook Up', 'That's When Your Heartaches Begin' HMV45POP359+
1957	'Loving You', 'Teddy Bear' RCA 45RCA1013+
1957	'Paralyzed', 'When My Blue Moon Turns To Gold Agin' HMV45POP378+
1957	'Got A Lot O' Livin' To Do', 'Party' RCA 45RCA1020+
1957	'Lawdy Miss Clawdy', 'Tryin' To Get To You' HMV45POP408+
1957	'Santa Bring My Baby Back', 'Santa Claus Is Back in Town' RCA 45RCA1025+
1957	'How Do You Think I Feel', 'I'm Left You're Right She's Gone' HMV45POP428
1958	'Jailhouse Rock', 'Treat

1960 'A Touch Of Gold': 'Hard Headed Woman', 'Good Rockin' Tonight', 'Don't', 'Teddy Bear' RCA 1045

1960 'A Touch Of Gold Vol 2': 'Wear My Ring Around Your Neck', 'Treat Me Nice', 'One Night', 'That's Alright' RCA 1048

1960 'Strictly Elvis': 'Old Shep', 'Any Place Is Paradise', 'Paralyzed', 'Is It So Strange' RCA 175

1960 'Such A Night': 'Such A Night', 'It Feels So Right', 'Like A Baby', 'Make Me Know It' RCA 190

LPs

1957 'Blue Suede Shoes', 'I Got A Sweetie (I Got A Woman)', 'I'm Counting On You', 'I'm Left You're Right She's Gone', 'That's Alright', 'Money Honey', 'Mystery Train', 'I'm Gonna Sit Right Down And Cry (Over You)', 'Tryin' To Get To You', 'One Sided Love Affair', 'Lawdy Miss Clawdy', 'Shake Rattle and Roll' HMV CLP 1093

1957 'Rock And Roll No 2': 'Rip It Up', 'Love Me', 'When My Blue Moon Turns To Gold Again', 'Long Tall Sally', 'First In Line', 'Paralyzed', 'So Glad You're Mine', 'Old Shep', 'Ready Teddy', 'Any Place Is Paradise', 'How's The World Treating You', 'How Do You Think I Feel' HMV CLP 1105

1957 'Mean Woman Blues', 'Teddy Bear', 'Loving You', 'Got A Lot O' Livin' To Do', 'Lonesome Cowboy', 'Hot Dog', 'Party', 'True Love' RCA 24001

1958 'Best Of Elvis': 'Heartbreak Hotel', 'I Don't Care If The Sun Don't Shine', 'Blue Moon', 'Tutti Frutti', 'All Shook Up', 'Hound Dog', 'Too Much', 'Anyway You Want Me', 'Don't Be Cruel', 'Playin' For Keeps' HMV DLP 1159

1958 'Santa Claus Is Back In Town', 'White Christmas', 'Here Comes Santa Claus', 'I'll Be Home For Christmas', 'Blue Christmas', 'Santa Bring My Baby Back', 'O Little Town of Bethlehem', 'Silent Night Holy Night', 'Peace In The Valley', 'I Believe', 'Take My Hand Precious Lord', 'It Is No Secret' RCA RD 27052

1959 'That's Alright', 'Lawdy Miss Clawdy', 'Mystery Train', 'Playin' For Keeps', 'Poor Boy', 'Money Honey', 'I'm Counting On You', 'My Baby Left Me', 'I Was The One', 'Shake Rattle And Roll', 'I'm Left You're Right She's Gone', 'You're A Heartbreaker', 'Tryin' To Get To You', 'Blue Suede Shoes' RCA RD 27120

1959 'A Date With Elvis': 'Blue Moon Of Kentucky', 'Milk Cow Blues Boogie', 'Baby Let's Play House', 'I Don't Care If The Sun Don't Shine', 'Tutti Frutti', 'I'm Gonna Sit Right Down And Cry', 'I Got A Woman', 'Good Rockin' Tonight', 'Is It So Strange', 'We're Gonna Move', 'Blue Moon', 'Just Because', 'One Sided Love Affair', 'Let Me' RCA RD 27128

1960 'Golden Records Vol. 2': 'I Need Your Love Tonight', 'Don't', 'Wear My Ring Around Your Neck', 'My Wish Came True', 'I Got Stung', 'Loving You', 'Teddy Bear', 'One Night', 'Jailhouse Rock', 'Treat Me Nice', 'A Big Hunk Of Love', 'I Beg Of You',

1960 'Elvis Is Back': 'Make Me Know It', 'Fever', 'The Girl Of My Best Friend', 'I Will Be Home Again', 'Dirty Dirty Feeling', 'The Thrill Of Your Life', 'Soldier Boy', 'Such A Night', 'It Feels So Right', 'The Girl Next Door', 'Like A Baby', 'Reconsider Baby' RCA RD 27171

1960 'G.I. Blues': 'What's She Really Like', 'Wooden Heart', 'Big Boots', 'Pocketful Of Rainbows', 'Blue Suede Shoes', 'Tonight Is So Right For Love', 'Frankfort Special', 'G.I. Blues', 'Shoppin' Around', 'Didja Ever', 'Doin' The Best I Can' RCA RD 27192.

SUN TRACKS

The following Sun recordings were released as singles in the States, but were not released in the U.K. HMV had Elvis re-make several of them when he moved from Sun and these were released over here in 1956 and 57.

1954 'That's Alright', 'Blue Moon of Kentucky', 'Good Rockin' Tonight', 'I Don't Care If The Sun Don't Shine'

1955 'You're A Heartbreaker', 'Milk Cow Blues Boogie', 'Baby Let's Play House', 'I'm Left You're Right She's Gone', 'Mystery Train', 'I Forgot To Remember To Forget'.

LLOYD PRICE

Lloyd was born on 9th March 1933, in New Orleans. Various members of his family were jazz and blues musicians, and his mother a gospel singer, and this gave him a strong musical awareness from an early age, which came to fruition during his high school days when he began to study the trumpet. Soon he found himself leading a five-piece band of school friends. They did local gigs and some spots on a New Orleans radio station which turned into a virtual residency, with Lloyd composing and the band performing station jingles and commercial break themes. One of these tunes, a bluesy 12-bar rocker called 'Lawdy Miss Clawdy' provoked tremendous listener interest and a barrage of requests for a recorded version, and it resulted in Lloyd and the band being signed by Art Rupe for his Speciality label. 'Clawdy' was recorded in a New Orleans studio with an uncredited Fats Domino pumping out the infectious piano arrangement, and was issued by Speciality to nationwide success in the rhythm and blues market. It was, in fact, one of the biggest-selling R & B discs of the year, 1952, and was to spawn cover versions by everybody from Elvis Presley down. Lloyd followed it with several other fair successes for Speciality, including 'Ooh Ooh Ooh', 'Ain't It A Shame', 'I Wish Your Picture Was You, and a self-answer disc entitled 'Forgive Me Clawdy'.

Lloyd was drafted into the army just when he seemed to have made a solid start in the music world, but he wasn't stopped from performing. Placed in the special services section, he organised another band from his fellow servicemen, and they toured the U.S. bases in the far east. Occasionally the band would back up other visiting singers; otherwise, Lloyd featured as vocalist, often using his own compositions: his beaty rewrite of the old American folk tune 'The Ballad Of Stack-O-Lee', which he called 'Stagger Lee', getting particularly good audience response.

He was discharged from the army in 1957 with the rank of sergeant, and immediately returned full-time to music. Together with an old friend, Harold Logan, who also became his personal manager, he began to write new material, and they set up a production company in Washington. The first result was 'Just Because' and 'Why', two self-compositions which Lloyd recorded with a new nine-piece group. The disc was leased to ABC-Paramount for release, and became an immediate pop hit, climbing to No. 29 in the Top 100 with a stay of almost five months.

It was well over a year later that Lloyd decided to record his service favourite 'Stagger Lee'. Released towards the end of 1958, it shot to a month's stay at No. 1 and a gold disc, and opened a period of really amazing popularity and consistent record sales. In 1959, Lloyd had two more million sellers in 'Personality' and 'I'm Gonna Get Married', and also entered the top twenty with 'Where Were You On Our Wedding Day?', 'For Love', 'Question' and 'No If's And Ands'. During this period, he was one of the most-played, most-booked and most busy artists on the R&B/rock'n'roll scene.

During the early sixties, Lloyd suffered a decline in chart success, but by this time was well enough established as a concert and cabaret entertainer to be able to take it in his stride. He started his own record label Double-L, which scored some chart success in 1963-64 with such artists as Wilson Picket, in his pre-'Midnight Hour' days. Lloyd himself also had a hit on Double-L at the end of 1963, when he updated the old standard 'Misty' and took it to No. 21.

Today, comparatively little is heard of Lloyd. He is, however, still recording, for Scepter/Wand, and has updated his style. No doubt he still earns enough royalties from the copyrights of 'Lawdy Miss Clawdy' and 'Stagger Lee' to see him securely into the foreseeable future.

BRITISH RELEASES TO 1960
+British Top 20 Hit

Singles

1957	'Just Because', 'Why' London 45HL8438
1958	'Stagger Lee', 'You Need Love' HMV45POP80+
1959	'Is It Really Love', 'Where Were You (On Our Wedding Day)' HMV45POP598+
1959	'Have You Ever Had The Blues', 'Personality' HMV45POP626+
1959	'I'm Gonna Get Married', 'Three Little Pigs' HMV45POP650+
1960	'Come Into My Heart', 'Won't You Come Home' HMV45POP672
1960	'Lady Luck', 'Never Let Me Go' HMV45POP712
1960	'For Love', 'No Ifs No Ands' HMV45POP741
1960	'If I Look A Little Blue', 'Question' HMV45POP772

Lloyd Price date unknown

1960   'Just Call Me', 'Who Coulda Told You' HMV45POP799

EPs

1959   'Lawdy Miss Clawdy', 'Where Were You (On Our Wedding Day)', 'Mailman Blues', 'Stagger Lee' HMV 5784

LPs

1959   'The Exciting Lloyd Price': 'Stagger Lee', 'I Wish The Picture Was Of You', 'Talking About Love', 'What Do You Do To My Heart', 'You Need Love', 'Mailman Blues', 'Where Were You (On Our Wedding Day)', 'Why', 'Lawdy Miss Clawdy', 'Oh Oh Oh', 'A Foggy Day',

'Just Because' HMV CLP 1285

1959   'Mr. Personality': 'Personality', 'Mary Anne', 'Time After Time', 'Have You Ever Had The Blues', 'Yakkety Yak Bing Bang', 'I Only Have Eyes For You', 'I'm Gonna Get Married', 'Dinner For One', 'Is It Really Love', 'Poppa Shun', 'All Of Me', 'I Want You To Know' HMV CLP 1314

1960   'Mr. Personality Sings The Blues': 'Ain't Nobody's Business', 'Please Send Me Someone To Love', 'Kidney Stew', 'I Cover The Waterfront', 'Talk To Me', 'I've Got The Blues

And The Blues Have Got Me', 'Just To Hold My Hand', 'Sittin' Here And Rockin', 'I Don't Need Nobody', 'Feelin' Lowdown', 'I'm A Lonely Man', 'Down For The Count' HMV CLP 1361

1960   'The Fantastic Lloyd Price': 'What Is This Thing Called Love', 'Blue Skies', 'Because Of You', 'Undecided', 'Let's Fall In Love', 'Don't Blame Me', 'In A Shanty In Old Shanty Town', 'Mean To Me', 'Don't Take Your Love From Me', 'Jeepers Creepers', 'Little Volcano', 'Five Foot Two Eyes of Blue' HMV CLP 1393

CLIFF RICHARD

Cliff was born Harry Webb on 14th October 1940, in Lucknow, India. His family moved to England when he was eight years old, and settled in Cheshunt, near London. At school, he developed an ambition to be a rock singer, and idolised Elvis. He became a clerk in an electrical goods factory at 15, but started to sing and play with various amateur rock and skiffle groups in the evenings and at weekends. Eventually, he formed a group called the Drifters with some friends, Terry Smart, Ken Pavey and Ian 'Sammy' Samwell, and they regularly played pubs and coffee bars in the West End, including the '2I's'.

At a talent show date at Shepherd's Bush Gaumont, where the group played a couple of times to rapturous teenage reaction, they were watched by an agent, George Ganjou, who had been persuaded by Sammy Samwell to come along. Ganjou was more impressed by the audience reaction than the music, and it was on the strength of this that he had the Drifters make a demo of two rock numbers, 'Breathless' and 'Lawdy Miss Clawdy', which he took to Norrie Paramout at EMI. While they were waiting for Paramor's verdict, the group quit their day jobs and accepted a summer season at Butlin's Holiday Camp at Clacton, where they were billed as 'Cliff Richard And The Drifters'. Harry's new stage name and separate billing were apparently suggested by an early business manager, Johnny Foster, who came up with 'Richard' rather than 'Richards' so that Cliff could always correct people who added the 's' to his name, and imprint it more firmly in their minds.

Meanwhile, Norrie Paramor had liked the demo, and after auditioning the group he decided to record them on a cover version of Bobby Helms' 'Schoolboy Crush'. For the B-side, he agreed to use a song which Ian Samwell had put together in a few hours : a strong rocker called 'Move It'. When the disc was released, in August 1958, 'Schoolboy Crush' quickly wilted and died, but 'Move It' began to get plays and attract attention, until at the end of September it entered the charts and began a rapid climb to its peak of No. 2. One pair of ears which were attracted very quickly belonged to T.V. producer Jack Good, who wanted Cliff for his new show 'Oh Boy', but wasn't too keen on taking the rest of the group. Tito Burns, who by now had become Cliff's Manager, persuaded him to do so, but in fact the Drifters themselves were unsure whether they could match up to the musical standards which were going to be demanded of them, and also whether they wanted to take the increased pressures of showbusiness. Eventually, with Cliff lined up for a spot on a nation-wide tour with the Kalin Twins, Pavey and Samwell decided to leave. To back him on the tour, Cliff brought in three musicians he had known from the '2 I's': Hank Marvin, Bruce Welch and Jet Harris.

At the end of 1958, a second single was released featuring another Ian Samwell rocker 'High Class Baby'. This followed 'Move It' into the Top Ten and climbed to No. 5, and both this and the next release, 'Livin' Lovin' Doll', which reached No. 20, featured the original Drifters line-up in the backing, having been recorded before the split.

Early in 1959, Terry Smart left the group and drummer Tony Meehan was brought in. The personnel of the Drifters had now changed completely, but in the new line-up remained stable for three years. With Marvin on lead guitar, Welch on rhythm, Harris on bass and Meehan drumming, Cliff now had a tight, assured professional group for both records and live appearances. The first recording they played on was 'Never Mind', which together with 'Mean Streak' gave Cliff his first double-sided chart success, both titles reaching the top 20 in May 1959.

By now, with five hits under his belt, a long and wildly successful 'Oh Boy' residency behind him, and his first LP 'Cliff', recorded live with the 'new' Drifters, an instant smash, Cliff was a star. He had already overtaken established favourites like Tommy Steele and Frankie Vaughan to become easily the biggest British teen idol in the country. He was given a small part in the Anthony Quayle film 'Serious Charge', and in this sang what was to be his biggest record success yet, 'Living Doll'.

'Doll' was a medium-tempo rockaballad, quite different from the wilder material which he had previously recorded, and Cliff didn't particularly care for the song. Its effect on the pop world was quite different, however. Within a couple of weeks it had shot to No. 1, where it remained for several weeks. What was more, it started to race up overseas hit parades as well — including the American Top 100 where it achieved the not inconsiderable

Cliff Richard, Oh Boy September 13 1958

position, for a British record in those days, of No. 30. By the end of the summer, the disc was a million seller.

Cliff had achieved his early ambition. He had reached the status of Britain's Elvis Presley, and was probably the highest-paid young entertainer in the country. The run of success of his records subsequent to 'Living Doll' underlines the fact: 'Travellin' Light' reached No. 1; 'A Voice In The Wilderness', from his second film 'Expresso Bongo', in which he had a major musical and dramatic role, No. 2; 'Fall In Love With You' No. 2; 'Please Don't Tease' No. 1; 'Nine Times Out Of Ten' No. 2; and 'I Love You, No. 2.

The Drifters, too, became infected with the magic touch. In 1959 they started to issue vocal records in their own right, but with no great success. Then in 1960, having changed their name to the Shadows to avoid confusion with America's R & B group the Drifters, they recorded a Jerry Lordan instrumental composition called 'Apache'. In August, this roared into the charts, displaced Cliff's own 'Please Don't Tease' at No. 1, and piled up hit placings around the world to earn a gold disc. The Shadows followed it with a stream ofinstrumental successes which rapidly established them as the world's top-selling group. Titles like 'Man Of Mystery', 'FBI', 'Kon-Tiki' and others gave them a seemingly endless list of top tenners.

The careers of Cliff and the Shadows through the 1960's and since is well-known and well-documented. They survived

Cliff Richard 1958

the U.K. beat group boom, the R&B boom, the folk-rock boom and anything else which happened to come along in pop music. Cliff made several hugely successful film musicals, and won more gold discs for 'The Young Ones', 'Bachelor Boy', 'Lucky Lips', 'It's All In The Game' and 'Congratulations'. The Shadows are now pursuing individual careers, but Cliff's popularity and star status are as inviolate as ever.

BRITISH RELEASES TO 1960
+British Top 20 Hit
Singles

1958 'Move It', 'Schoolboy Crush' Columbia 45DB4178+
1958 'High Class Baby', 'My Feet Hit The Ground' Columbia 45DB4203+
1958 'Livin' Lovin' Doll', 'Steady With You' Columbia 45DB4249
1959 'Mean Streak', 'Never Mind' Columbia 45DB4290+
1959 'Apron Strings', 'Livin' Doll' Columbia 45DB4306+
1959 'Dynamite', 'Travelling Light' Columbia 45DB4351+
1960 'A Voice In The Wilderness', 'Don't Be Mad At Me' Columbia 45DB4398+
1960 'Fall In Love With You', 'Willie And The Hand Jive' Columbia 45DB4431+
1960 'Please Don't Tease', 'Where Is My Heart' Columbia 45DB4479+
1960 'Nine Times Out Of Ten', 'Thinkin' Of Our Love' Columbia 45DB4506+
1960 ' D' In Love', 'I Love You' Columbia 45DB4507+
EPs
1959 'Serious Charge': 'Living

Doll', 'No Turning Back', 'Mad About You', 'Chinchilla' Columbia 7895
1959 'Cliff No. 1': 'Apron Strings', 'My Babe', 'I Got A Feeling', 'Baby I Don't Care', 'Jet Black' Columbia 7903
1959 'Cliff No. 2': 'Donna', 'Move It', 'Ready Teddy', 'Too Much', 'Don't Bug Me Baby', 'Driftin'' Columbia 7769
1959 'Expresso Bongo': 'Love', 'A Voice In The Wilderness', 'The Shrine On The Second Floor', 'Bongo Blues' Columbia 7783
1959 'Cliff Sings No. 1': 'Here Comes Summer', 'I Gotta Know', 'Blue Suede Shoes', 'The Snake And The Bookworm' Columbia 7788
1959 'Cliff Sings No. 2': 'Twenty Flight Rock', 'Pointed Toe Shoes', 'Mean Woman Blues', 'I'm Walkin'' Columbia 7794
1960 'I'll String Along With You', 'Embraceable You', 'As Time Goes By', 'The Touch Of Your Lips' Columbia 7808
1960 'I Don't Know Why', 'Little Things Mean A Lot', 'Somewhere Along The Way', 'That's My Desire' Columbia 7816
1960 'Cliff's Silver Discs': 'Please Don't Tease', 'Fall In Love With You', 'Nine Times Out Of Ten', 'Travelling Light' Columbia 8050
1960 'Me And My Shadows No. 1': 'I'm Gonna Get You', 'You And I', 'I Cannot Find A True Love', 'Evergreen Tree', 'She's Gone' Columbia 7837

1960 'Me And My Shadows No. 2': 'Left Out Again', 'You're Just The One To Do It', 'Lamp Of Love', 'Choppin' And Changin', 'We Have Made It' Columbia 7841

LPs
1959 'Apron Strings', 'My Babe', 'Down The Line', 'I Got A Feeling', 'Baby I Don't Care', 'Donna', 'Move It', 'Ready Teddy', 'Too Much', 'Don't Bug Me Baby', 'That'll Be The Day', 'Danny', 'Whole Lotta Shakin' Goin' On', 'Jet Black', 'Driftin'', 'Be Bop A Lula' Columbia 33SX 1147
1959 'Cliff Sings': 'Blue Suede Shoes', 'The Snake And The Bookworm', 'I Gotta Know', 'Here Comes Summer', 'Twenty Flight Rock', 'Pointed Toe Shoes', 'Mean Woman Blues', 'I'm Walkin'', 'I'll String Along With You', 'Embraceable You', 'As Time Goes By', 'The Touch Of Your Lips', 'Little Things Mean A Lot', 'I Don't Know Why', 'Somewhere Along The Way', 'That's My Desire' Columbia 33SX 1192
1960 'Me And My Shadows': 'I'm Gonna Get You', 'You And I', 'Evergreen Trees', 'I Cannot Find A True Love', 'She's Gone', 'Left Out Agin', 'You're Just The One To Do It', 'Lamp Of Love', 'Workin' After School', 'Choppin' And Changin'', 'We Have It Made', 'Gee Whiz Tell Me It's You', 'Tell Me', 'I Love You So', 'I'm Willing To Learn', 'I Don't Know' Columbia 33SCX 3330

LITTLE RICHARD

Little Richard was born as Richard Wayne Penniman on 5th December 1932, (not 25th December 1935, as the various record blurbs will have you believe,) in Macon, Georgia, the fourth child of what was to become quite a large family of 14. The Pennimans were extremely poor, and at about the age of 7, Richard and his sister were singing and dancing on the streets of Macon for pennies to supplement the family income.

Coming from a very religious family, Richard joined the local Church choir, and taught himself to play the organ, but he soon lost this job, as even in those days he rocked up the music too much for his elders. He later left home, reputedly turned out by his father on account of his long hair and raucous singing, his father preferring Bing Crosby and the like. He then joined several travelling medicine shows, where he hiked the various patent medicines and pills for about $2 a day. His travels brought him to Atlanta, Georgia, in 1951, where a last minute decision got him entering a talent contest, with a prize of a recording contract with RCA Victor. He won it, and cut eight rather insignificant sides of blues-type material, which didn't sell very well. His journeys, still with the medicine shows, brought him to Houston, Texas, where he signed a contract with Don Robey of Peacock Records during 1953, and cut eight sides for him, again insipid material. Several sides featured the Johnny Otis Orchestra, on other sides he formed part of a group called the Tempo Toppers.

Whilst still under contract with Robey he met up with Lloyd Price, who already had several million sellers for the Speciality label, and Price persuaded Richard to send him a demo tape: a very badly recorded tape of a gospel song called 'He's My Star'. The then producer for Speciality, Bumps Blackwell, listened to the song and felt that Richard had something, but because the label was having so much success, with many hit artists, Richard's tape was forgotten for almost twelve months. Eventually, Art Rupe, President of Speciality, was persuaded by Bumps to give the tape a listen, and Richard was sent a plane ticket for New Orleans, where Speciality records were made. It was found that Richard was still under contract to Peacock, but Don Robey was persuaded to give up the contract for $600!

In October 1955 the first session took place. The songs included 'Wonderin' Directly From My Heart', 'All Night Long', 'I'm Just A Lonely Guy'. During a break for refreshments, Richard began playing the piano, and started singing a song he had written himself: 'Tutti Frutti'. Bumps Blackwell, who was producing the session, felt the song was strong, that the lyrics Richard was using were too sexually explicit, so he sent for a girl he knew who could write acceptable lyrics; one Dorothy La Bostrie. Richard didn't want to sing the song in front of her, but was finally persuaded to do it. Afterwards they carried on with the session, and just 15 minutes before their time was up, Dorothy came in with the lyrics, and it took just 3 takes to make.

'Tutti Frutti' was his first million seller and was quickly followed by others, in fact many of his records became double sided hits, including 'Long Tall Sally', 'Slippin' And Slidin''; 'Ready Teddy', 'Rip It Up'; 'She's Got It', 'Heebie Jeebies'; 'Jenny Jenny', 'Miss Ann'. All his records for Speciality were made within a twelve month period. Art Rupe wanted Richard to come in and record some more, but he wouldn't; the only thing he got was another demo tape, which Richard and his band had recorded at a Baltimore Radio station. It was 'Keep A Knockin'', which was originally less than a minute long. Rupe stretched it in the studio and it became another million seller.

In 1957 Richard embarked on a tour of Australia, then suddenly announced to a dismayed public that he was going to retire. On his return to the States he enrolled in Oakwood College in Alabama to study Theology. Richard retired from concert appearances for five years, but cut a number of albums of gospel material for Mercury, 20th Century Fox, Atlantic. Plus four extremely good rock'n'roll songs for an obscure label called Little Star, which he recorded under his group's name of 'The Upsetters', these were recorded circa 1960, and were the first rock'n'roll records he had cut since 1956. The titles were 'I'm In Love Again', 'Every Night About This Time', 'Freedom Ride', 'Valley Of Tears'. Unfortunately they received little promotion, and were only local hits.

He came out of retirement in 1962, and embarked on a tour of England. It was a huge success,

Little Richard, Peacock publicity photo, c. 1953

and his gospel recording of 'He Got What He Wanted' reached the lower parts of the British charts. He returned to U.K. in 1963 and brought with him a 16 year old organ player, by the name of Billy Preston. Richard intended to sing gospel on this tour, but was persuaded otherwise by the promoter. Concurrently, he marked his return to the Speciality label with a rocker entitled 'Bama Lama Bama Loo', which smashed into the British charts. He also made a T.V. Spectacular for Granada, which it was in every sense of the word. An hour long programme saw Richard hammer out all his great hits, accompanied by the British outfit, Sounds Incorporated.

Richard returned for yet another successful tour in 1966. But record-wise his career was in a decline. He had left Speciality after his success with 'Bama Lama', and signed for Vee-Jay, he cut a lot of rehashes of his old hits, plus a few new things, but most of them were pretty dreadful. The label went bust towards the end of 1965, and he signed for the Los Angeles based label Modern, where he cut a lot of sides, none of them very successful, and quit the label only about five months after joining them. He then joined Okeh, and cut a lot of Soul material, with little chart success. In 1968 he joined Brunswick, where he had less success than ever; he only cut three discs in 12 months. He left Brunswick in mid-1969, and

didn't sign with anyone until early 1970, when he joined Reprise. In 1972 at Wembley Stadium, his camp antics outraged many of his old fans in the audience and he was actually booed.

BRITISH RELEASES TO 1960
+British Top 20 Hit

Singles

Nov 56	'Ready Teddy', 'Rip It Up' London 45HL08336
Feb 57	'Long Tall Sally', 'Tutti Frutti' London 45HL08366+
Mar 57	'She's Got It', 'The Girl Can't Help It' London 45HL08382+
July 57	'Lucille', 'Send Me Some Lovin ' London 45HL08446+
Sep 57	'Jenny Jenny', 'Miss Ann' London 45HL08470+
Dec 57	'Can't Believe You Wanna Leave', 'Keep A Knockin ' London 45HL08509
Mar 68	'Good Golly Miss Molly', 'Hey-Hey-Hey-Hey' London 45HL08560+
July 58	'Ooh My Soul', 'True Fine Mama' London 45HL8647
Dec 58	'Baby Face', 'I'll Never Let You Go' London 45HL08770+
Mar 59	'By The Light Of The Silvery Moon', 'Early One Morning' London 45HLU8831+
June 59	'Kansas City', 'She Knows How To Rock' London 45HLU8868
Feb 60	'Baby', 'I Got' London 45HLU9065

EPs

| 1957 · | 'She's Got It', 'I'm Just A Lonely Guy', 'Heebie |

1957 Jeebies', 'Slippin' And Slidin ' London 1071
'Rip It Up', 'Ready Teddy', 'Long Tall Sally', 'Tutti Frutti' London 1074

1958 'Lucille', 'Send Me Some Lovin ', 'The Girl Can't Help It', 'Jenny Jenny' London 1103

1958 'Miss Ann', 'Oh Why', 'Can't Believe You Wanna', 'Baby' London 1106

1959 'Baby Face', 'By The Light Of The Silvery Moon', 'She Knows How To Rock', 'Early One Morning' London 1208

1959 'Keep Rockin ', 'Good Golly Miss Molly', 'All Around The World', 'True Fina Mama' London 1234

1960 'Kansas City', 'Shake A Hand', 'Chicken Little Baby', 'Whole Lotta Shakin' Goin' On' London 1235

LPs

1958 'Tutti Frutti', 'True Fine Mama', 'Can't Believe You Wanna Leave', 'Ready Teddy', 'Baby', 'Slippin' And Slidin ', 'Long Tall Sally', 'Miss Ann', 'Oh Why', 'Rip It Up', 'Jenny Jenny', 'She's Got It' London HAO 2055

1959 'Keep A Knockin ', 'By The Light Of The Silvery Moon', 'Send Me Some Lovin ', 'I'll Never Let You Go', 'Heebie Jeebies', 'All Around The World', 'Good Golly Miss Molly', 'Baby Face', 'Hey-Hey-Hey-Hey', 'Ooh My Soul', 'The Girl Can't Help It', 'Lucille' London HAU 2126

1960 'Shake A Hand', 'Chicken Little Baby', 'All Night Long', 'The Most I Can Offer', 'Lonesome And Blue', 'Wonderin', 'She Knows How To Rock', 'Kansas City', 'Directly From My Heart', 'Maybe I'm Right', 'Early One Morning', 'I'm Just A Lonely Guy', 'Whole Lotta Shakin' Goin' On' London HA-U 2193

1960 'Ain't Nothin' Happenin ', 'Why Did You Leave Me', 'Every Hour', 'I Brought It All On Myself', 'Taxi Blues', 'Get Rich Quick', 'Please Have Mercy On Me', 'Thinkin' About My Mother', 'Crazy Lips', 'Any Hour', 'Hey Operator', 'That's A Lot Of Brass' (With Buck Ram Rock'n'Roll Orchestra) Camden CDN 125

SINGLES NOT RELEASED IN U.K.

Little Richard did not have any records released in the U.K. till 1956 but prior to that time a considerable amount of material was released in the U.S.A. These recordings are listed below. Serial numbers refer to American pressings.

1951 approx.
'Taxi Blues', 'Every Hour' RCA Camden 4392
'Get Rich Quick', 'Thinkin' About My Mother' RCA Camden 4582
'Ain't Nothing Happening', 'Why Did You Leave Me' RCA Camden 4772

'I Brought It All On Myself', 'Please Have Mercy On Me' RCA Camden 5052
During the same period RCA Camden also released two EP's and 1 LP:
'Every Hour', 'Ain't Nothin' Happenin ', 'Why Did You Leave Me', 'I Brought It All On Myself' RCA Camden CAE 411
'Taxi Blues', 'Please Have Mercy On Me', 'Get Rich Quick', 'Thinkin' About My Mother' RCA Camden CAE 446
'Ain't Nothin' Happenin', 'Why Did You Leave Me', 'Every Hour', 'I Brought It All On Myself', 'Taxi Blues', 'Get Rich Quick', 'Please Have Mercy On Me', 'Thinkin' About My Mother', remaining tracks by Buck Ram and His Rock and Roll Band RCA Camden CAL 420

1954 approx.
'Fool At The Wheel', 'Ain't That Good News' : Duces of Rhythm and Tempo Peacock 1616
'Rice Red Beans And Turnip Greens', 'Always' : Toppers , Richard Lead Vocal Peacock 1628
'Little Richard Boogie', 'Directly From My Heart' : Little Richard with the Johnny Otis Orchestra. Peacock 1658
'Maybe I'm Right', 'I Love My Baby': Little Richard with the Johnny Otis Orchestra. Peacock 1673
'I Love My Baby', 'Directly From My Heart' also released on Vogue EP VEP 170-155 with remaining tracks by Memphis Slim.

1956 on
Richard's British releases in the fifties, on London, were taken from his U.S. Speciality recordings and London did not release all of them over here. Here are the ones we didn't hear as singles:
'Tutti Frutti', 'I'm Just A Lonely Guy' Speciality 561

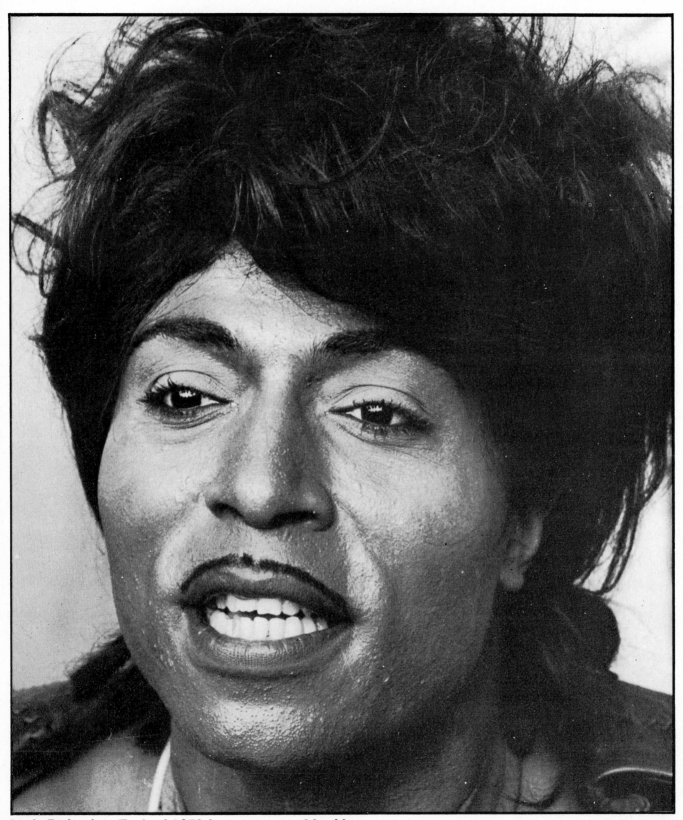

Little Richard, in England 1972 for a concert at Wembley

'Long Tall Sally', 'Slippin' And Slidin ' Speciality 572
'She's Got It', 'Heebie Jeebies' Speciality 584

'Girl Can't Help It', 'All Around The World' Speciality 591
'Early One Morning', 'She Knows How To Rock' Speciality 652

'By The Light Of The Silvery Moon', 'Wonderin ' Speciality 660
'Kansas City', 'Lonesome And Blue' Speciality 664.

JACK SCOTT

Although little known in Britain Jack Scott was one of the best white rock and rollers coming out of New York from 1957 to 1960. Unfortunately most of his rock material was released on the B sides of his records and consequently few people in Britain, or the States, were aware of his strength as a rock and roller, and his chart successes were mainly ballads.

He was born in Windsor, Ontario, on 24th January 1938 of Italian/American immigrant parents and his real name was Jack Scafone. His family moved to Detroit when he was only a few years old and it was over the Detroit radio stations that he first heard country music; Hank Williams became his first musical love and Jack started playing country guitar when he was 8. By the time he was sixteen he had his own group called the Southern Drifters, playing local dances and record hops.

In 1956 he made a demo of two of his own songs, 'My True Love' and 'Leroy', the latter being about a friend of his who had been jailed for street fighting. Jack took the demo to various local talent scouts and after a few weeks it was heard by Joe Carlton, producer for ABC-Paramount in New York. Carton signed him immediately and recorded four songs with him which were released during 1957, on two singles: neither was a chart success. The two A sides were superb rockabilly though, 'Baby She's Gone' and 'Two Timin' Woman'. 'Two Timin' Woman' marked the debut of Jack's regular backup vocal group the Chantones, who stayed with him till 1962.

Carlton wasn't put off by the lack of success, however, and when he started his own label in 1958 he bought Scott's contract and master tapes from ABC. 'My True Love' backed with 'Leroy' was the first Scott release for Carlton and both sides entered the American Top 50, selling a million copies in little over a month.

T.V. and radio exposure followed and the next five releases also made the charts in the States, even though Scott was drafted into the army until 1960. He narrowly failed to have a million seller with the haunting 'Goodbye Baby'. His final Carlton release, 'I Never Felt Like This', left the charts in 1959 and marked the end of a period of twelve months when he was consistently in the hit parade.

His subsequent records lacked the special quality Joe Carlton was able to bring out and it is for the B sides from the Carlton period that rock and roll fans remember him; these singles, together with 'Go Wild Little Sadie', this one being released on a 1958 Carlton EP, arguably rank among the finest white rock and roll of the period.

On leaving the services in 1960 Jack's contract was bought by Top Rank (USA). His first recording for them, a country ballad called 'What In The World's Come Over You', became his second gold disc, and he followed it with a third, another balled called 'Burning Bridges'. A further three singles and three albums, one of them a tribute to Hank Williams, were issued until in 1961 he was signed to Capitol when Rank pulled out of the record business.

Capitol launched a series of singles, some from the Rank masters they had acquired, and the first three gained some chart success. However, by 1962 he began to slide and no further recordings were issued in Britain apart from a Capitol LP made up of single tracks in 1964. During late 1963 he joined Groove, a subsidiary of RCA, and recorded some genuine rock and roll again, but with little success. In 1965 he was transferred to RCA but after three unsuccessful country and pop releases his contract was terminated. From then until late 1970 he made only sporadic recordings for ABC, Jubilee and finally GRT.

Since then little has been heard of him. He still lives in Detroit and continues to perform in local clubs and rock revival packages.

BRITISH RELEASES TO 1960

Singles

1958	'Leroy', My True Love' London HLU8626
1958	'With Your Love', 'Geraldine' London HLU8765
1958	'Goodbye Baby', 'Save My Soul' London HLU8804
1959	'I Never Felt Like This', 'Bella' London HLL8851
1959	'The Way I Walk', 'Midgie' London HLL8912
1959	'There Comes A Time', 'Baby Marie' London HLL8970
1960	'What In The World's Come Over You', 'Baby Baby' Rank JAR280
1960	'Cool Water', 'It Only Happened Yesterday' Rank JAR 419
1960	'Patsy', 'Old Time Religion' Rank JAR 524

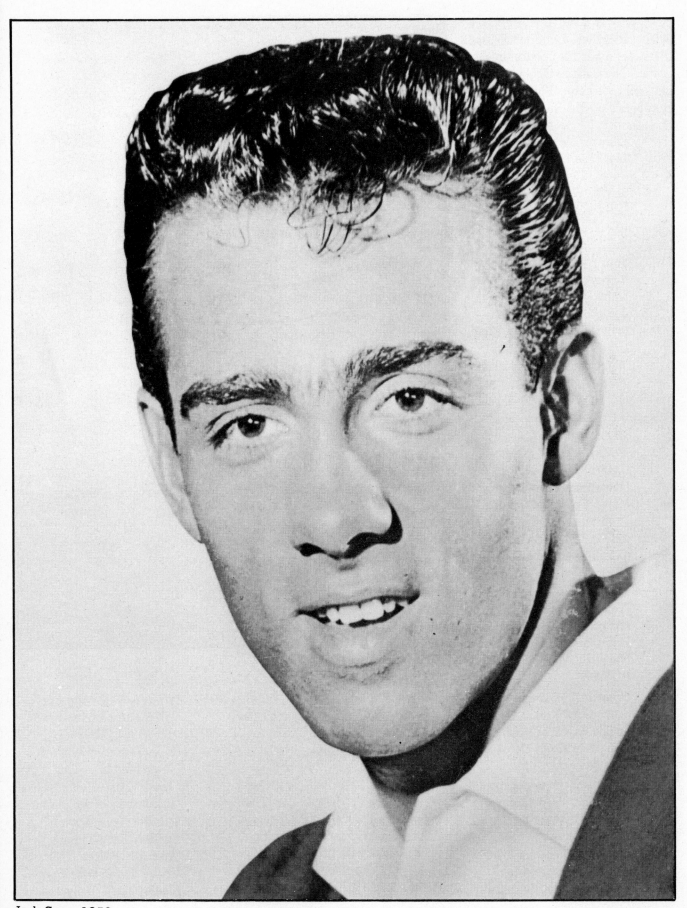

Jack Scott 1958

N.B. It is these London releases that were made for Carlton in the States. One Carlton single was not released over here: 'Five Little Numbers', 'Just A Summer Love' Carlton 485.

EPs

1959 'My True Love': 'My True Love', 'Leroy', 'Goodbye Baby', 'With Your Love' London RE 1205

LPs

1958 'Jack Scott': 'Save My Soul', 'With Your Love', 'Leroy', 'No One Will Ever Know', 'Geraldine', 'I Can't Help It', 'Indiana Waltz', 'Midgie', 'My True Love', 'The Way I Walk', 'I'm Dreaming Of You', 'Goodbye Baby' London HA-L 2156

1960 'I Remember Hank Williams': 'My Heart Would Know', 'Your Cheating Heart', 'I Could Never Be Ashamed Of You', 'Cold, Cold Heart', 'You Win Again', 'Half As Much', 'They'll Never Take Her Love From Me', 'Crazy Heart', 'I'm Sorry For You My Friend', 'Take These Chains From My Heart', 'I Can't Escape From You', 'May You Never Be Alone' Top Rank BUY 034

1960 'What In The World's Come Over You?': 'What In The World's Come Over You', 'My King', 'It's My Way Of Loving You', 'Burning Bridges', 'Baby Baby', 'So Used To Loving You', 'Cruel World', 'Good Deal', 'Lucille', 'Window Shopping'. Rank 25/024

1960 'The Spirit Moves Me': 'Down By The Riverside',

Neil Sedaka in the early 1960's

'Old Time Religion', 'The Gospel Train', 'I Wanna Be Ready', 'Just A Closer Walk With Thee', 'He'll Understand', 'When The Saints', 'Swing Low Sweet Chariot', 'Ezekial Saw The Wheel', 'Joshua Fit The Battle Of Jericho', 'Little David, Play Your Harp', 'Roll, Jordan, Roll' Top Rank 35/109

1960 'What Am I Living For?': 'What Am I Living For?', 'Go Wild Little Sadie', 'Baby Marie', 'Bella', 'I Never Felt Like This', 'There Comes A Time', 'Baby She's Gone', 'You Can Bet Your Bottom Dollar', 'Two-Timin' Woman', 'I Need Your Love', 'Hank Williams Medley' U.K. Unissued.

NEIL
SEDAKA

Neil Sedaka was born on 13th March 1939, in Brooklyn, New York. His grandmother had been a concert pianist, and Neil's taxi-driver father was determined that his son should develop in the same direction. Whilst at Lincoln High School in Brooklyn, he studied piano and composition, and played on Arthur Rubinstein's radio programme 'Musical Talent In Our Schools', which led to a two-year piano scholarship at the Juillard School of Music.

His pop career started almost by accident through his songwriting. He had been writing songs as a sideline during his high school days, and many were used in school productions, or performed by the school and summer camp bands which Neil formed and directed. After leaving school, he teamed up with lyricist Howard Greenfield, an old classmate, and they began to produce songs together, quickly coming to the attention of publisher Don Kirshner and his colleague Al Nevins, who signed the partnership to a writing contract. Kirshner introduced them to Connie Francis, and they wrote 'Stupid Cupid' for her; her first rock'n'roll hit, and a world-wide smash. Then a demo of Neil singing one of the team's songs himself was sent to Steve Sholes at RCA-Victor, primarily to try to interest him in the song as possible material for one of his artists. Sholes, however, was more interested in the voice on the disc, recognising immediate commercial appeal. In no time at all, Neil had a second contract, with RCA as a singer.

The first single released was 'The Diary', a Sedaka/Greenfield composition as was practically every one of Neil's succeeding hits, which went straight into the U.S. charts at the end of 1958, and reached No. 14. The follow-up, a really pounding rocker titled 'I Go Ape', was less of a success there, reaching only 42. In England, however, it really caught on, reaching No. 9 in the charts.

Neil's next hit was his first million-seller, and the song with which he is still best associated today: the classic 'Oh Carol'. This reached No. 9 in the U.S. and No. 3 in Britain, and established him indelibly on the scene, paving the way for a four-year run of consistent hitmaking on both sides of the Atlantic. The discs were mainly beat ballads like 'Oh Carol', with the occasional rocker and a couple of slowies: 'Stairway

To Heaven', 'You Mean Everything To Me', 'Calendar Girl', 'Little Devil', 'Happy Birthday', 'Sweet Sixteen', 'Breaking Up Is Hard To Do', 'Next Door To An Angel', and 'Alice In Wonderland'; all these were U.S. Top 20 hits between 1960 and 1963. 'Breaking Up' was a No. 1 and a million-seller, while 'Calendar Girl' and 'Sweet Sixteen' also won gold discs. Smaller chart successes came with 'Run Samson Run', 'Sweet Little You', 'King of Clowns', 'Let's Go Steady Again', 'The Dreamer' and 'Bad Girl', and these, apart from the last two, were British hits as well.

After 'Bad Girl', which reached No. 33 in the U.S.A., Neil seemed to lose his magic touch with startling suddenness. The reason was almost certainly that this time coincided with the 1964 invasion of the U.S. charts by the

Beatles and other British artists, when American record buyers ignored most of their own artists almost entirely.

A drop from the limelight did comparatively little harm to Neil's career, however. He continued his songwriting, devoted more time to his serious music studies, and generally rested. Also, RCA did not drop his contract and he continued to record; 'The World Through A Tear' and 'The Answer To My Prayer', were minor hits later in the sixties. Finally, the last couple of years have brought a major revival of interest in him, firstly as a songwriter again, Tony Christie's 'Amarillo' et al, and then once more as a disc artist; in a slightly updated, Randy Newman-ish bag, but retaining the ever-distinctive Sedaka sound. Recent chart successes with 'Beautiful You', 'That's When The Music Takes Me. and the revived 'Oh Carol' suggest that Neil has a way to go yet.

BRITISH RELEASES TO 1960
+British Top 20 Hit
Singles

1958	'No Vacancy', 'The Diary' RCA 45RCA1099
1959	'I Go Ape', 'Moon Of Gold' RCA 45RCA1115+
1959	'Crying My Heart Out For You', 'You Gotta Learn Your Rhythm And Blues' RCA 45RCA1130
1959	'Oh Carol', 'One Way Ticket' RCA 45RCA1152+
1959	'Ring A Rockin'., 'Fly Don't Fly On Me' London HLW8961
1960	'Forty Winks', 'Stairway To Heaven' RCA 45RCA1178+
1960	'You Mean Everything To

Tommy Steele on location in a Bermondsey coffee bar 1957

Me', 'Run Samson Run' RCA 45RCA1198

1960 'Calendar Girl', 'The Same Old Fool' RCA 45RCA1220+

EPs

1959 'You Gotta Learn Your Rhythm And Blues', 'Crying My Heart Out For

You', 'I Go Ape', 'The Diary' RCA 166

1960 'Another Sleepless Night', 'I Ain't Hurtin' No More', 'Stairway To Heaven', 'Forty Winks Away' RCA 186

LPs

1959 'You're Knockin' Me Out',

'The Diary', 'I Ain't Hurtin' No More', 'Stupid Cupid', 'All I Need Is You', 'I Waited Too Long', 'Fallin', 'Another Sleepless Night', 'I Go Ape', 'Moon Of Gold', 'I Belong To You', 'As Long As I Live' RCA RD 27140

TOMMY STEELE

Tommy Steele, born in Bermondsey, was Britain's first home-grown answer to Elvis Presley, our own 'Rock'n'Roll' star. Of course, there were Englishmen playing rock music during 1955/56; unconvincingly like Don Lang and Tony Crombie, but no equivalent to Elvis, Carl Perkins, Gene Vincent, etc.; somebody who was young, looked good, and could sing rock'n'roll.

During 1956, Tommy was a merchant seaman, a steward on board a transatlantic luxury liner. He sang for his crewmates from time to time, because he could play the guitar and sing, and possessed a remarkably infectious personality, but he had never really considered singing for a living. However, whenever his ship docked in London, Tommy would trek over to the 2 I's coffee bar in Soho, where it was the custom for regular customers to provide the 'cabaret', as it were; the owner would persuade the budding rock and skiffle singers who frequented the place to perform for each other. Tommy was a regular there, and since the 2 I's was a regular pitch for record company talent scouts, it was only a matter of time before he was noticed. He was snapped up for a three-year contract with Decca and booked for a string of concert dates virtually before he could kiss the merchant navy goodbye! Britain had its Elvis Presley. Incidentally the original owner of the 2 I's was Paul Lincoln who later became the outrageous masked wrestler, Doctor Death.

In October 1956, immediately after he had signed his contract, Tommy recorded his first single 'Rock With The Cavemen', and a group named the Steelmen was formed to back him on disc and stage. The record raced into the charts, and quickly achieved its peak of No. 13. It was followed just six weeks later by another release, this time a cover version of a U.S. hit by Guy Mitchell, 'Singing The Blues'. The Mitchell version hit the British charts with a bang and sailed into the No. 1 slot in the first week of 1957, but the Steele disc bounded up in its wake, came to rest one position behind, and then astounded everybody by actually capturing the top spot from the original! If there had been any doubt during his meteoric rise about Tommy Steele's star status, there was none now. He topped bills all over the country, went into cabaret in

London at the Cafe De Paris, and most amazing of all, started a film of his own life story, liberally dressed up with songs to make it a semi-musical!

In February 1957, Tommy issued another single, cheekily covering Guy Mitchell's own follow-up, 'Knee Deep In The Blues'. This time, however, he was not so successful in competition, reaching only No. 15 while Mitchell went on into the top 3. After this, maybe because of it, he left cover discs alone for a while. His next hit was a Lionel Bart song written for the film 'The Tommy Steele Story', a loping beat ballad called 'Butterfingers'. Released to coincide with the film, it made the top 10 and spent nearly four months in the charts, the start of a very consistent run of hits. 'Shiralee' came next, then a Top 10-riding double sider, 'Water

Water', 'Handful Of Songs'. This coupling reached No. 5 in another long stay, and the 'Handful' side rapidly became Tommy's signature tune on stage and T.V. He followed it with a minor hit in 'Hey You', and then another massive one with 'Nairobi', which went to No 3. A second successful film, a musical comedy titled 'The Duke Wore Jeans', also appeared at this time.

By now, the beginning of 1958, several other British rockers had sprung up in Tommy's wake. Artists like Jim Dale, Terry Dene and Marty Wilde were meeting with varying degrees of success, and the spotlight was moving away from Steele, the original cockney rocker. However, he kept the hits coming, and took 'Happy Guitar', 'The Only Man On The Island', and a cover of Ritchie Valens' 'Come On Let's Go' into the top 20 in the wake of 'Nairobi'.

1959 saw almost the last of Tommy's big hits. By now, people like Cliff Richard and Marty Wilde were attracting more teenage fans, and Tommy was already starting to shake off the mantle of a rock'n'roller in favour of an 'all-round' showbiz career. His third film 'Tommy The Toreador' helped demonstrate this point, as did the Top 10 hit which came from it, 'Little White Bull', a singalong number with a kiddie chorus. His other hit of the year, though, was more in the old rock groove, a cover of Freddy Cannon's 'Tallahassie Lassie'.

'What A Mouth' in 1959 was Tommy's last Top 10 hit; it was almost a music-hall number, an uptempo show-type comedy song. He went into pantomime, into general variety, and into musicals via the highly successful 'Half A Sixpence'. By 1962 his move from pop to showbiz was complete. Later years have seen him as a Broadway success, in 'Half A Sixpence', and as the Hollywood star of 'The Happiest Millionaire'.

BRITISH RELEASES TO 1960
+British Top 20 Hit
Singles
1956 'Rock Around The Town', 'Rock With The Cavemen' Decca 45F10795+

1956 'Doomsday Rock', 'Elevator Rock' Decca 45F10808

1956 'Rebel Rock', 'Singing The Blues' Decca 45F10819+

1957 'Knee Deep In The Blues', 'Teenage Party' Decca 45F10849+

1957 'Butterfingers', 'Cannibal Pot' Decca 45F10877+

1957 'Grandad's Rock', 'Shiralee' Decca 45F10896+

1957 'A Handful Of Songs', 'Water Water' Decca 45F10923+

1957 'Hey You', 'Plant A Kiss' Decca 45F10941

1958 'Happy Guitar', 'Princess' Decca 45F10976+

1958 'Nairobi', 'Neon Sign' Decca 45F10991+

1958 'It's All Happening', 'What Do You Do' Decca 45F11026

1958 'I Puts The Light On', 'The Only Man On The Island' Decca 45F11041

1958 'Come On Lets Go', 'Put A Ring On Her Finger' Decca 45F11072+

1958 'A Lovely Night', 'Marriage Type Love' Decca 45F11089

1958 'Hiawatha', 'The Trial' Decca 45F11117

1959 'Give Give Give', 'Tallahasee Lassie' Decca 45F11152+

1959 'You Were Mine', 'Young Ideas' Decca 45F11162

1959 'Little White Bull', 'Singing Time' Decca 45F11177+

1960 'Kookaburra', 'What A Mouth (What A North And South)' Decca 45F11245+

1960 'Happy-Go-Lucky-Blues', 'The Girl With The Long Black Hair' Decca 45F11275

1960 'Boys And Girls', 'Must Be Santa' Decca 45F112299
EPs
1957 'Young Love', 'Doomsday Rock', 'Wedding Bells', 'Rock With The Cavemen' Decca 6388

1957 'Singing The Blues', 'Rebel Rock', 'Knee Deep In The Blues', 'Elevator Rock' Decca 6389

1957 'Take Me Back Baby', 'Water Water', 'Will It Be You', 'Build Up' Decca 6398

1957 'A Handful Of Songs', 'Cannibal Pot', 'Time To Kill', 'You Gotta Go' Decca 6424

1958 'Photograph', 'Hair Down Hoe Down', 'Princess', 'Happy Guitar' Decca 6472

1958 'Come On Let's Go', 'Put A Ring On Her Finger', 'The Only Man On The Island', 'Number Twenty Two Across The Way' Decca 6551

1959 'I'm A Little Blackbird Looking For A Bluebird', 'Georgie On My Mind', 'Sweet Georgia Brown', 'Mandy Make Up Your Mind' Decca 6592

1959 'Tommy The Toreador Soundtrack': 'Tommy The Toreador', 'Take A Ride', 'Where's The Birdie', 'Little White Bull', 'Singing Time', 'Amanda'

Decca 6607

1960 'What A Mouth', 'Kookaburra', 'Hollerin' And Screamin ', 'Little Darlin ' Decca 6660
LPs
1957 'Tommy Steele Stage Show': 'Giddy Up A Ding Dong', 'Treasure Of Love', 'Honky Tonk Blues', 'Razzle Dazzle', 'Kaw-liga', 'Teenage Party', 'Wedding Bells', 'What Is This Thing Called Love', 'On The Move', 'Rock With The Cavemen' Decca LF 1287

1957 'Tommy Steele Story': 'Butterfingers', 'Cannibal Pot', 'Take Me Back Baby', 'I Like', 'A Handful Of Songs', 'You Gotta Go', 'Water Water', 'Will It Be You', 'Two Eyes', 'Build Up', 'Time To Kill', 'Elevator Rock', 'Doomsday Rock', 'Teenage Party' Decca LF 1288

1957 A song called 'Butterfly' is included on the compilation LP 'All Star Hit Parade No. 2' Decca F10915

1958 'The Duke Wore Jeans Soundtrack': 'It's All Happening', 'What Do You Do', 'Family Tree', 'Happy Guitar', 'Hair Down Hoe Down', 'Princess', 'Thanks A Lot', 'Photograph' Decca LF 1308

1960 'Get Happy With Tommy': 'Hollerin' And Screamin ', 'Lonesome Traveller', 'A Handful Of Songs', 'Nairobi', 'Little Darlin ', 'Old Obadiah', 'What A Mouth', 'Shiralee', 'Kookaburra', 'Tommy The Toreador', 'Shout', 'So Long (It's Been Good To Know Yuh)' Decca LK 4351

Tommy Steele with Cliff Richard

CONWAY TWITTY

Twitty was born in Mariano, Arkansas, on 1st September 1935, his real name being Harold Jenkins. 'Conway Twitty' was given to him by his agent early in his career, from a combination of place names on a road map.

Harold grew up amidst a strong country music milieu. His father was a ferry pilot on the Mississippi who sang and played the guitar in his spare time, and the youngster had guitar lessons from him early in childhood. He was a proficient enough entertainer by the age of ten to have made broadcasts on a local radio station, and at twelve he formed a teenage C&W band called the Phillips Country Ramblers, playing the usual round of hops and barndances in his hometown area.

He was drafted into the army in the early fifties, and posted to Tokyo. He formed a service group called the Cimmarons and did a stint of forces entertaining, including his own radio programme. At this time his repertoire was wholly C&W, but rock'n'roll was starting to make its influence felt by the time of Conway's discharge in 1956, and once back in the States, it was not long before he travelled to Memphis to audition with Sam Phillips at Sun.

Twitty's stay at Sun was a frustrating one, for although Phillips showed interest at first and a lot of material was recorded, none of it ever got as far as being issued on disc. Phillips seemed content to keep the songs as demos for other artists, and some were used in this way; Roy Orbison, for example, recorded 'Rockhouse'. A somewhat disillusioned Conway left Memphis and went to Mercury in Nashville, where he was again signed up and recorded, this time with some positive results. Several singles featuring strong rock performances were issued and sold reasonably well, but only one made any kind of national impact. This was 'I Need Your Lovin'', which briefly grazed the U.S. charts at No. 93 in May 1957.

By 1958, Twitty had changed labels again, moving this time to MGM. He was virtually the first rocker on the label, and not unnaturally was promoted, in much the same way as Gene Vincent had been by Capitol, as

MGM's own particular 'answer' to Elvis Presley. He cut his own composition 'It's Only Make Believe' in a rather exaggerated Presley ballad style, building at the end to a grand climax. Its impact was immediate; by the end of the year, the disc had reached No. 1 in both the American and British charts, and had sold well over a million.

Conway started 1959 as a rock'n'roll star, much in demand for T.V. spots and tours, and already in line for a film role; he made his debut in 'Sexpot Goes To College'. The year also provided him with a run of further hits in the U.S. charts: 'The Story Of My Love', No. 28; 'Hey Little Lucy' No. 87; 'Mona Lisa' No. 29; and 'Danny Boy' No. 29. In Britain 'Hey Little Lucy' made the top 20, and 'Mona Lisa' climbed to No. 6, boosted by a brief visit here and an appearance on Jack Good's 'Oh Boy'.

In 1960, Conway's U.K. sales slumped somewhat, despite a successful tour, but in the States

he went from strength to strength. 'What Am I Living For?', 'Is A Bluebird Blue?', and 'A Whole Lotta Shakin' Goin' On' all carved up the charts, while 'Lonely Blue Boy', a rewrite of 'Danny', the unissued song from Elvis' 'King Creole', reached No. 5 and brought another gold disc. More film parts came along too, in 'Rich, Young And Deadly' and 'College Confidential'. In fact, Conway's wave of success lasted him into 1962 before finally falling, and considered overall, his consistency during this three-years-plus period was exceptional. Only towards the end did a drop in his record sales become really apparent, and this was after scoring yet another top 30 entry with 'C'est Si Bon' in late 1961.

As the sixties moved on, it became apparent to Twitty that he was not going to recapture his glory in the pop field, where he was rapidly becoming regarded as a left-over from the fifties. He took the same course as Jerry Lee Lewis, and turned his attention fully back to the straight country and western music which had been his roots. A mid-60's label change to Decca, which was extremely strong in the country market, helped tremendously. Over the course of the next five years, Twitty became one of the most consistently successful, popular, and highly-paid artists in the field, with a list of smash hits in the C&W charts even longer than that of his pop hits. He will still occasionally perform some of his oldies on stage, especially in Europe, where audiences still clamour for them, but he has committed himself entirely to the

Conway Twitty, date unknown

music he loves best, and perhaps his rocker days were 'only make believe' after all.

BRITISH RELEASES TO 1960
+British Top 20 Hit

Singles

1957 'Maybe Baby', 'Shake It Up' Mercury MT173

1958 'I'll Try', 'It's Only Make Believe' MGM

45MGM992+

1958 'Make Me Know You're Mine', 'The Story Of My Love' MGM 45MGM1003

1959 'Hey Little Lucy', 'When

I'm Not With You' MGM 45MGM1016+

1959 'Heavenly', 'Mona Lisa' MGM 45MGM1029+

1959 'Halfway To Heaven', 'Rosaleena' MGM 45MGM1047

1959 'Lonely Blue Boy', 'My One And Only' MGM 45MGM1056

1960 'What Am I Living For', 'The Hurt In My Heart' MGM 45MGM1066

1960 'Is A Blue Bird Blue', 'She's Mine' MGM 45MGM1082

1960 'Tell Me More', 'What A Dream' MGM 45MGM1095

1960 'Don't You Dare Let Me Down', 'C'est Si Bon' MGM 45MGM1118

EPs

1959 'It's Only Make Believe': 'It's Only Make Believe', 'I'll Try', 'Will You Love Me Then As You Love Me Now', 'I Vibrate' MGM 684

1960 'Hey Little Lucy': 'Hey Little Lucy', 'When I'm Not With You', 'The Story Of My Love', 'Make Me Know You're Mine' MGM 698

1960 'Saturday Night With Conway Twitty': 'Blueberry Hill', 'She's Mine', 'Hey Miss Ruby', 'Restless' MGM 719

1960 'I Need Your Lovin'': 'Shake It Up', 'Maybe Baby', 'I Need Your Lovin'', 'Double Talk' Mercury 10069

1960 'Is A Bluebird Blue': 'Is A Bluebird Blue', 'The Hurt In My Heart', 'What Am I Living For', 'She's Mine' MGM 45 MGM738

Ritchie Valens 1958

LPs

1959 'It's Only Make Believe', 'Hallelujah I Love Her So', 'First Romance', 'Make Me Know You're Mine', 'Sentimental Journey', 'I Vibrate', 'The Story Of My Love', 'I'll Try', 'You'll Never Walk Alone', 'Don't You Know', 'My One And Only You', 'Mona Lisa' MGM C781

1959 'Saturday Night With Conway Twitty': 'Rosaleena', 'Heavenly', 'She's Mine', 'Blueberry Hill', 'Hey Little Lucy', 'Halfway To Heaven', 'Hey Miss Ruby', 'You Win Again', 'Restless', 'Beachcomber', 'Judge Of My Heart', 'Goin' Home' MGM C801

1960 'Lonely Blue Boy': 'Lonely Blue Boy', 'Just Because', 'Easy To Fall In Love', 'Sorry', 'My Adobe Hacienda', 'A Huggin' And A Kissin'', 'Trouble In Mind', 'Eternal Tears', 'Blue Moon', 'Can't We Go Steady', 'Heartbreak Hotel' MGM C829

RITCHIE VALENS

Ritchie Valens, real name Richard Venezuela, was born on 13th May 1941 in Pacoima, Los Angeles. His family was of Mexican origin, and Ritchie grew up with a strong exposure to Spanish and Mexican music and folksong, learning to play the Spanish guitar during his early years at school.

Ritchie attended Pacoima High School as a teenager, and here he formed a group called the Silhouettes, which played at school dances and shows. By now he had developed a distinctive style of his own: a mixture of rock'n'roll and traditional Mexican rhythms which had tremendous drive and fire. He became so popular locally that his name caught the ear of Bob Keene, a record producer who owned the Del Fi label in Hollywood. Keene gave Ritchie an audition, was impressed, and signed him to a contract with Del Fi. This was in 1958, when Ritchie was barely 17.

The first record they cut was a Valens composition entitled 'Come On, Let's Go', a powerful rocker. It was released in the late summer of 1958 and became an almost immediate success, climbing to No. 42 in the U.S. Top 100 and staying in the charts for three months. Keene and Ritchie looked around for a follow-up, and came up with a coupling of two very different numbers. The first, 'Donna', was a slow, melancholy ballad sung in the currently fashionable 'pleading' tone. It was another self-composition, the title being the name of Ritchie's girlfriend, Donna Ludwig. The flip was 'La Bamba', a traditional Mexican song adapted by Ritchie, and sung in Spanish. The arrangement was an exhilarating marriage of wild flamenco and rock; an irresistible dance rhythm. However, the number was apparently only recorded after repeated pressuring by Bob Keene; Valens himself thought that he was doing the old song a disservice by revamping it in this way.

'Donna' broke first at the beginning of December, 1958. Early in the new year, it had catapulted into the Top 10 and came to rest with a lengthy stay at No. 2, selling over a million copies. It might have reached No. 1, had not a sizeable number of disc jockeys and record buyers discovered 'La Bamba'. Entering the charts in January 1959, this became a simultaneous smash hit in its own right and climbed to No. 22. Ritchie became a rock sensation and entered the usual round of concerts, T.V. spots and package tours. At the end of January 1959, it seemed that he was assured of a glistening career ahead, but it was not to be.

Ritchie was playing on the same nation-wide package tour as Buddy Holly and The Big Bopper in February, and with them he took the charter plane at Fargo, North Dakota, on the night of 3rd February. The aircraft crashed in a blizzard, and everyone in it was killed. The story goes that the tour artists had drawn lots for the limited number of places on the plane, and that when Ritchie's name came up, he remarked: 'Gee! That's the first time I've ever won anything in my life!'

BRITISH RELEASES TO 1960
+British Top 20 Hit

Singles

Feb 59	'Donna', 'La Bamba' London 45HL8803+
Mid 59	'Come On Let's Go', 'Dooby Dooby Wah' Pye 7N2500
June 59	'Bluebird Over the Mountains', 'That's My Little Suzie' London 45HL8886

Gene Vincent, in the Granada TV show Whole Lotta Shakin Goin On
1965

GENE VINCENT

Gene was born in February, 1935 in Norfolk, Virginia, his real name being Gene Vincent Craddock. He shot to fame in mid-1956 with his own composition 'Be-Bop-A-Lula', a distinctive rocker which has since been re-recorded by almost every other artist in the rock field. It reached No. 9 in the U.S. charts and No. 17 in Britain, and was lip-synched by Gene and his group the Blue Caps in the film 'The Girl Can't Help It'. The Blue Caps consisted of Cliff Gallup, guitar, Willie Williams, guitar, Jack Neal, bass, and Dickie Harrell, drums, with the later additions and replacements of Bobby Jones, bass guitar, Johnny Meeks, guitar, and second vocalist Paul Peek.

Gene had acquired a recording contract after winning a Capitol talent contest, the main purpose of which had been to hurriedly find their own version of Elvis Presley. In retrospect, however, it is easy to see that they found something completely different. Vincent had little of Presley's teenage sex appeal, and his record sales after the gold disc-winning 'Lula' quickly declined: another Top 20 hit with 'Lotta Lovin'', and three smaller hits with 'Bluejean Bop', 'Race With The Devil' and 'Dance To The Bop', and he'd had his day as far as the charts were concerned. However, the quality of his material never declined, and Gene's reputation remained high amongst those who gradually came to value rock'n'roll for its own qualities, and were little concerned whether the singer had a pretty hairstyle.

Commercially, much of Gene's material, his stage act, and his appearance worked against him. His song lyrics tended to be well in advance of their time, often overtly sexual, ('Woman Love' for example,) and caused raised eyebrows and down-turned thumbs amongst the American radio programmers. Moreover he was a partial cripple, with a troubled leg which dogged him painfully until his death. He would appear on stage clad in black leather, in a frozen stance which looked downright menacing and hunched over the microphone with his thin, drawn face apparently undecided whether to give in to misery on one hand or his personal agony on the other. One leg would be bent at a permanent angle, the other stretched as if cast in iron. He would grasp the mike stand as though it kept him from collapse, and rock back and forward with it. Then he would purge himself with a rock performance which used up every ounce of his being. Vincent was like a Rock Hamlet; he was too real for his day, and it is now very clear just how much he really was living a tragedy.

Unsurprisingly, the end of Gene's story was not a happy one. He worked with some success throughout the rest of the fifties and the sixties, largely because of his popularity in Britain and Europe, where he was widely appreciated for never turning his back on the style of music and the material which had first brought him fame. He was involved in the 1959 car crash which killed Eddie Cochran, and sustained heavy injuries himself. Eventually, he became completely immersed in the figure of mental and physical agony which he projected on stage. Capitol let his long-term contract run to completion, but the impression is that they held the door open and then breathed a relieved sigh after booting him through it. A period with Challenge Records, who tried to switch him to C&W, and an embarrassingly bad 'come-back' in 1969 on John Peel's Dandelion label, did nothing for Gene except finally turn some of the fans of his Capitol rock material away from him. He became an unreliable performer, a booker's risk, a truly tragic figure in his last live performances, which were painful in every sense. Eventually, he died of a bleeding ulcer in Los Angeles, on the 12th October 1971.

BRITISH RELEASES TO 1960
+British Top 20 Hit

Singles

1956	'Be Bop A Lula', 'Woman Love' Capitol 45CL14599+
1956	'Gonna Back Up Baby', 'Race With The Devil' Capitol 45CL14628
1956	'Bluejean Bop', 'Who Slapped John' Capitol 45CL14637+
1957	'Jumps Giggles And Shouts', 'Wedding Bells' Capitol 45CL14681
1957	'Crazy Legs', 'Important Words' Capitol 45CL14693
1957	'B-i-bickey--bi, bo-bo-go', 'Five Days Five Days' Capitol 45CL14722
1957	'Lotta Lovin'', 'Wear My Ring' Capitol 45CL14763
1958	'Dance To The Bop', 'I Got It' Capitol 45CL14808
1958	'I Got A Baby', 'Walkin' Home From School' Capitol 45CL14830
1958	'Baby Blue', 'True To

1958 'Rocky Road Blues', 'Yes I Love You Baby' Capitol 45CL14908

1958 'Git It', 'Little Love' Capitol 45CL14935

1958 'Be Bop Boogie Boy', 'Say Mama' Capitol 45CL14974

1959 'Over The Rainbow', 'Who's Pushing Your Swing' Capitol 45CL15000

1959 'Frankie And Johnny', 'Summertime' Capitol You' Capitol 45CL14868

45CL15035

1959 'Right Now', 'The Night Is So Lonely' Capitol 45CL15053

1959 'Right Here On Earth', 'Wild Cat' Capitol 45CL15099

1959 'I've Got To Get You Yet', 'My Heart' Capitol 45CL15115

1960 'Pistol Packin' Mama', 'Weeping Willow' Capitol 45CL15136+

1960 'Ac-cent-tchu-ate The Positive', 'Anna-Annabelle'

Capitol 45CL15169

1960 'Jezebel', 'Maybe' Capitol 45CL15179

1960 'If You Want Me Lovin'', 'Mister Lordiness' Capitol 45CL15185

EPs

1958 'Dance To The Bop', 'Be Bop A Lula', 'Lotta Lovin ', 'Well I Knocked And I Knocked' Capitol T1009

1959 'Hot Rod Gang': 'Dance In The Street', 'Baby Blue', 'Lovely Loretta', 'Dance

Gene Vincent with Jet Harris c. 1963

1960 'Five Feet Of Lovin ', 'The Wayward Wind', 'Somebody Help Me', 'Keep It A Secret' Capitol 1059

1960 'I Love You', 'Peace Of Mind', 'Summertime Blues', 'Look What You Gone And Done To Me' Capitol 3-1059

LPs

1957 'Bluejean Bop', 'Who Slapped John', 'Ain't She Sweet', 'I Flipped', 'Waltz Of The Wind', 'Jump Back Honey Jump Back', 'Wedding Bells (Are Breaking Up That Old Gang Of Mine)', 'Jumps Giggles And Shouts', 'Up A Lazy River', 'Bop Street', 'Peg Of My Heart' Capitol T764 1958

1958 'Red Blue Jeans and A Pony Pony Tail', 'Hold Me Hug Me Rock Me', 'Unchained Melody', 'You Told A Fib', 'Cat Man', 'You Better Believe', 'Cruisin'', 'Double Talkin' Baby', 'Blues Stay Away From Me', 'Pink Thunderbird', 'I Sure Miss You', 'Pretty Pretty Baby' Capitol T811

1958 'Gene Vincent Rocks': 'Brand New Beat', 'By The Light Of The Silvery Moon', 'You'll Never Walk Alone', 'Frankie And Johnny', 'In My Dreams', 'Flea Brain', 'Rollin' Danny', 'You Belong To Me', 'Your Cheatin' Heart', 'Time Will Bring You Everything', 'Should I Ever Love Again', 'No Lie' Capitol T790

1959 'Record Date': 'Five Feet of Lovin'', 'The Wayward

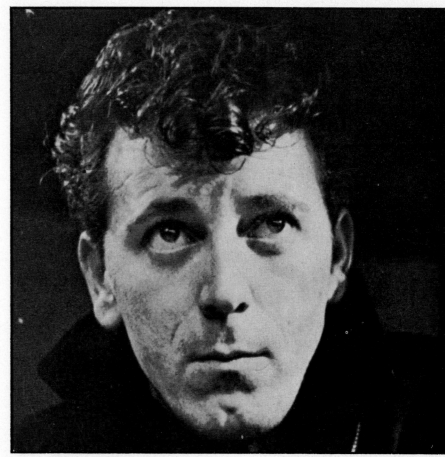

Gene Vincent 1960

Wind', 'Somebody Help Me', 'Keep It A Secret', 'Hey Good Lookin'', 'Git It', 'Teenage Partner', 'Peace Of Mind', 'Look What You Gone And Done To Me', 'Summertime', 'I Can't Help It', 'I Love You' Capitol T1059

1960 'Sounds Like Gene Vincent': 'My Baby Don't Low', 'I Can't Believe You Want To Leave', 'I Might Have Known', 'In Love Agin', 'You Are The One For Me', 'Ready Teddy', 'I Got To Get You Yet', 'Vincent's Blues', 'Maybe', 'Now Is The Hour', 'My Heart', 'Maybelline' Capitol T1207

1960 'Crazy Times': 'Crazy

Times', 'She She Little Sheila', 'Darlene', 'Everybody's Got A Date But Me', 'Why Don't You People Learn To Drive', 'Green Back Dollar', 'Big Fat Saturday Night', 'Mitchiko From Tokyo', 'Hot Dollar', 'Ac-cent-tchu-ate The Positive', 'Blue Eyes Cryin' In The Rain', 'Pretty Pearly', 'The World Is A Beautiful Waltz' Capitol ST1342

MARTY WILDE

Marty was born Reginald Smith, his stage name coming from promoter Larry Parnes, who found him singing and playing a guitar in a London coffee bar early in 1957. It was a familiar beginning for many of the artists who appeared on the British rock scene: many of them got no further than the coffee bar, but Marty, like Tommy Steele before him and Cliff Richard soon after, was one of the lucky ones. Larry Parnes took him under contract, put him on some touring shows and got him some T.V. spots, which were soon followed by a recording contract with Philips. His first release was a cover version of Jimmie Rodgers' 'Honeycomb', a disc with a strong folk flavour, which contrasted somewhat with the rock material he had been doing on stage, but nevertheless seemed to suit his light, expressive voice. But it wasn't a hit, and neither were the two follow-ups 'Love Bug Crawl' and 'Oh Oh, I'm Falling In Love Again'.

The breakthrough came with Marty's fourth disc, which was a cover version of Jody Reynolds' 'Endless Sleep', a doomy ballad with an intriguing death orientated lyric. It entered the charts midway through July 1958, and climbed slowly but steadily until it reached a peak of No. 4 during September. It finally left the Top Thirty towards the end of October, by which time it had sold upwards of 200,000 copies and Marty was a star, with a weekly residency on Jack Good's new T.V. show 'Oh Boy'. He had two minor hits with 'Misery Child' and a cover of Dion & The Belmonts' 'No-One Knows', which took him into 1959, the year of his greatest success.

Marty had three gigantic hits during 1959, all with covers of American million-sellers. 'Donna', originally recorded by Ritchie Valens, reached No. 4, 'A Teenager In Love', Dion and the Belmonts again, made No. 2, and 'Sea Of Love', covered from Phil Phillips, No. 3. Marty became virtually a permanent feature on T.V. in 'Oh Boy', 'Drumbeat' and 'Boy Meets Girls', on which he acted as host and compere. He had a girls' magazine named after him, appeared in a film acting role for the first time in 'Jet Storm', and did a spot on the Royal Variety Show. His first album, 'Wilde About Marty', was also released, and featured a variety of performances, including several out-and-out rockers like 'Down The Line', 'Splish Splash' and 'Mean Woman Blues'.

1960 opened with him in the Top 10 again, with 'Bad Boy', for the first time a self-composed song. To most people's amazement, it also caught on in the U.S.A., where it climbed to No. 45 in the Top 100, a truly astounding feat for a British disc at that time. Marty travelled to the States, visited Hollywood and Vegas, appeared on several networked T.V. shows, and went to New York for his first American recording session. However, he made little lasting impression on the U.S., and returned home to find his British stature slightly diminished too. Cliff Richard and Adam Faith were carving up the charts between them, and the sales of several previously-established hitmakers were suffering noticeably by comparison. Marty's next few records: 'Johnny Rocco', 'Johnny At The Crossroads' and 'Angry', made virtually no impression. It was not until the end of the year that one of the numbers he had recorded in America, 'Little Girl', returned him to the Top 20.

In 1961, the decision was taken to attempt to broaden Marty's appeal into other sides of show business. He went to South Africa to film a straight acting part in the film 'The Hellions', and went to the West End of London on his return to take the role of Conrad Birdie in the stage musical 'Bye Bye Birdie'. Effectively, he was turning his back on the record world, and probably wisely; the fans who had given him three top tenners during 1959 had moved on to newer idols. However, this did not prevent Marty from having two fair-sized hits during 1961 with a cover version of Bobby Vee's 'Rubber Ball' and later with 'Tomorrow's Clown'.

He made the Top 20 for the last time during the summer of 1962 with a good revival of Frankie Laine's 'Jezebel', and scraped the Top 30 during November with 'Ever Since You Said Goodbye'. A 1963 appearance in the film 'What A Crazy World' kept him in the public eye for a little longer, but the mass public had lost interest, and Marty went into the northern club circuit during the 60's, and finally into songwriting and production. He's currently grooming his son, Ricky Wilde, for teenybopper superstardom.

+BRITISH RELEASES TO 1960
British Top 20 Hit
Singles
1957 'Honeycomb', 'Wild Cat'

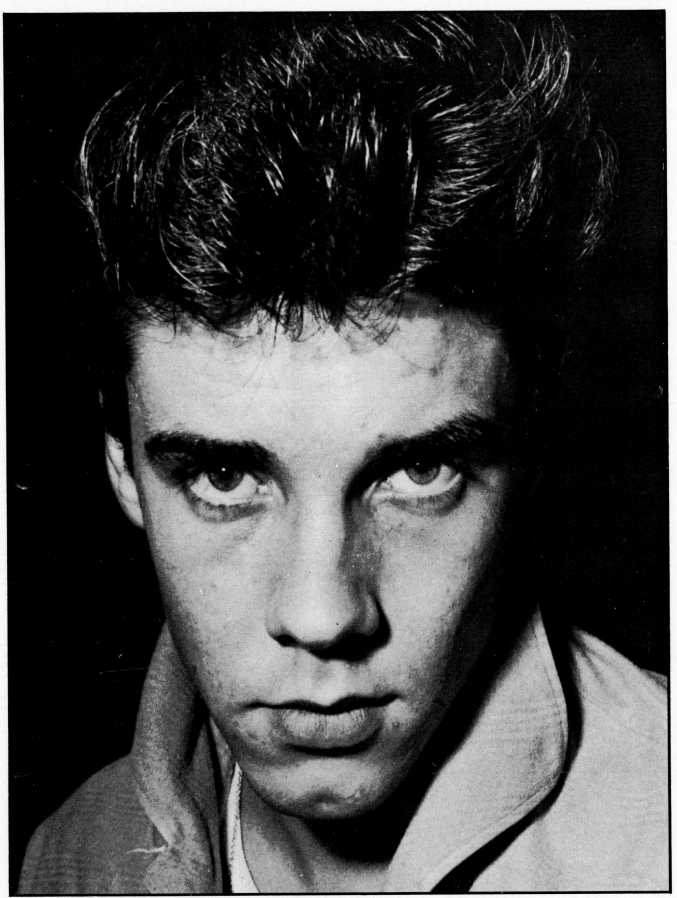

Marty Wilde 1958

Philips PB750
1957 'Afraid Of Love', 'Love
Bug Crawl' Philips PB781
1957 'Oh Oh I'm Falling In
Love Again', 'Sing Boy
Sing' Philips 45PB804

1958 'Endless Sleep, 'Her Hair
Was Yellow' Philips
45PB835+
1958 'Misery's

Child, 'My Lucky Love'
Philips 45PB850
1958 'No One Knows', 'The Fire
Of Love' Philips 45PB875
1959 'Donna', 'Love-A Love-A
Love-A' Philips PB902+
1959 'A Teenager In Love',
'Danny' Philips 45PB926+
1959 'Sea Of Love', 'Teenage
Tears' Philips 45PB959+
1959 'Bad Boy', 'It's Been So
Nice' Philips 45PB972+
1960 'Johnny Rocco', 'My
Heart And I' Philips
45PB1002
1960 'Johnny At The
Crossroads', 'The Fight',
Philips 45PB1022
1960 'Angry', 'I Wanna Be
Loved By You' Philips
45PB1037
1960 'Little Girl', 'Your
Seventeenth Spring'
Philips 45PB1078+
1960 'Like Making Love',
'Rubber Ball' Philips
45PB1101+

EPs
1957 'Wild Cat', 'Honeycomb',
'Love Bug Crawl', 'Afraid
Of Love' Philips 12164
1958 'More Of Marty': 'Oh Oh
I'm Falling In Love Again',
'Sing Boy Sing', 'Her Hair
Was Yellow', 'Endless
Sleep' Philips 12200
1959 'Sea Of Love': 'Teenage
Tears', 'Sea Of Love',
'Danny', 'A Teenager In

Marty Wilde

Love' Philips 12327
1960 'The Versatile Mr. Wilde':
'Come On-A My House',
'Please', 'Alone', 'Autumn
Leaves' Philips 12385
1960 'Marty Wilde Favourites':
'Little Girl', 'Your
Seventeenth Spring',
'Rubber Ball', 'Like
Making Love' Philips
12422
LPs
1959 'Wilde About Marty':
'Down The Line', 'Put Me
Down', 'Love Of My Life',
'Blue Moon Of Kentucky',
'I Flipped', 'You've Got
Love', 'Dream Lover', 'All
American Boy', 'Mean
Woman Blues', 'Are You
Sincere', 'High School
Confidential', 'Don't Pity
Me', 'Splish Splash', 'So
Glad You're Mine' Philips

BBL 7342
1960 'Marty Wilde Showcase':
'Bad Boy', 'Johnny
Rocco', 'Teenage Tears',
'Sea Of Love',
'Honeycomb', 'No One
Knows', 'The Fire Of
Love', 'Endless Sleep', 'A
Teenager In Love', 'My
Heart And I', 'Donna', 'It's
Been So Nice' Philips BBL
7380
1960 'The Versatile Mr. Wilde':
'Cutting Loose', 'Alone',
'Johnny At The
Crossroads', 'The Fight',
'Try A Little Tenderness',
'Amapola', 'I Wanna Be
Loved By You', 'Come
On-A My House', 'Is This
A Dream', 'Please', 'To Be
With You', 'Autumn
Leaves' Philips BBL 7385

LARRY WILLIAMS

Larry Williams was born in New Orleans on 10th May, 1935. When he was still fairly young, his family moved to California, and Larry grew up in Oakland and Berkeley He took up piano and guitar in his teens, and played both instruments in a couple of local groups, the Teardrops and the Lemon Drops, neither of which achieved much in the way of commercial success. When the second broke up during 1954, Larry went solo as a singer/pianist, but continued with only minor success until he met Lloyd Price. Price was still riding high in the wake of his 'Lawdy Miss Clawdy' hit for Speciality, and needed a pianist for his band. Williams' pounding style fitted perfectly, and Larry was signed, playing continuously with Price until the latter was drafted into the army, and then continuing at Speciality as a session musician.

In 1957, Larry came to the attention of Art Rupe, Speciality's owner. Rupe was engaged in a search for more talent in the style of Little Richard, then chalking up a series of massive hits for the label, to give him another major performer in the rock'n'roll world, and once again Larry's own piano and vocal style stood him in good stead. He signed a contract and cut a disc, 'Just Because', ironically a cover version of a number just issued by his old boss Lloyd Price, who was now with another label. It was Lloyd's version of the song which sold, however, and Larry turned to a composition of his own, 'Short Fat Fanny', as a follow-up. This was a raver with strong Little Richard overtones, and featured a neat lyric gimmick: the titles of many of the most popular rock hits of the previous two years. It caught on quickly, entered the U.S. top 100 in June, 1957 and stayed there for five months, rising to No. 6 and collecting a gold disc.

At about this time, Little Richard announced his retirement from show business, and Larry became Speciality's biggest rock attraction. He cut 'Bony Moronie', another of his own songs, and this too was a major and long-running Top 20 success. The flip, 'You Bug Me Baby, was almost equally popular, and made the charts in its own right. 'Bony Moronie' was also a hit in Britain, reaching No. 11 early in 1958.

After this, Larry's sales began to decline. Why, it is difficult to imagine, since his 1958 releases were pure rock classics: 'Dizzy Miss Lizzy', 'Slow Down', 'She Said Yeah', and 'Bad Boy', all numbers revived in the 1960's by the Beatles and the Stones. Possibly a fall from favour of the harder rocking sounds and the rise of glossier productions at this time in the U.S.A. was the reason for Larry's decline. His later Speciality discs like 'Steal A Little Kiss' and 'Give Me Love' seemed to be attempts to come to grips with these changes, but he was to find no more commercial success.

In the mid-sixties, there was a brief revival of interest in Larry, in England, at least. A couple of early hits were reissued, he came to London for some successful live appearances, and also cut a live L.P. of his greatest hits for the Sue label. When the Beatles cut 'Slow Down', and later 'Bad Boy' and 'Dizzy Miss Lizzy' as L.P. tracks, there was a renewed seeking out of the original versions, but by then Larry had moved on into a relatively minor role in the general R&B/Soul field, and eventually he dropped from sight. Whatever he's doing in 1973, few people know about it.

BRITISH RELEASES TO 1960
+British Top 20 Hit

Singles

Sept 57	'High School Dance', 'Short Fat Fanny' London 45HLN8472
Jan 58	'Bony Moronie', 'You Bug Me Baby' London 45HLU8532+
May 58	'Dizzy Miss LIzzy', 'Slow Down' London 45HLU8604
May 59	'I Can't Stop Loving You', 'Steal A Little Kiss' London 45HLU8911
1960	'Baby Baby', 'Get Ready' London 45HLM9053

EPs

1959	'I Was A Fool', 'Peaches And Cream', 'Hotchy Koo', 'The Dummy' London 1213

Larry Williams, date unknown

LINK WRAY

Link Wray only had one record released in Britain in the fifties, 'Rumble', his only American hit in the period also. It would be hard to overestimate the importance of that record in the history of rock and roll. It had a similar effect on young musicians as Elvis' first records had on young record buyers: mammoth and revolutionary. Pete Townshend, to name one, has said: 'If it hadn't been for Link Wray and 'Rumble' I would never have picked up a guitar'.

'Rumble' had strong cultural links with the blues style of New Orleans but its sound was completely original. Heavy tremolo and a dirty, primitive treatment of the melody effectively evoked an image of a teenage gang on the prowl.

Link was born in 1929 in North Carolina, part of a family with strong Shawnee Indian roots. He started playing guitar when he was 8, picking up tips from a neighbouring black 'blues' musician who would come round to the Wray home.

He was in the army from 1950 to 1952, getting a lung blown out in Korea in the process. On his return to the States, and after a period of convalescence, Link started playing professionally in small clubs and dance halls. And it was at one of these dances that 'Rumble' was born. 'I was playing in a record hop in Fredericksburg, Virginia, back in 1957 and somebody asked for a 'stroll'. I didn't know one so I just started playing and the kids really dug it. It wasn't like the usual chinka-chinka-chinka rock and roll stuff. People kept asking for it so we did the record the next year.'

Actually, it wasn't that simple. Link made a demo of 'Rumble' and this received some airplay on a Washington radio station. The D.J. responsible, Bill Grant, played the demo to Archie Bleyer of the Cadence record label. Bleyer in fact didn't like the record but agreed to put it out in order to swing some other deal he was working on. So 'Rumble' eventually came out on Cadence; this would be around early 1958. But Bleyer never had any faith in Link's music and released him from his contract after only a year.

The next label Link signed to was Epic who he stayed with until 1962, making a series of records, 'Rawhide' and others, most of which were mechanical derivations of 'Rumble' and which depressed him greatly. In 1962 he signed with Swan, making 'Weekend and 'Jack The Ripper', but a year later the label went out of existence.

By this time Link was so disenchanted with the record business that he vowed never to record again. He carried on playing in clubs though, making just enough money to get by.

Meanwhile the Wray family moved to Accokeek, where he and his brothers built a very primitive recording studio in a chicken coop on their land. They called it the Shack and over the next few years made many tapes there. In 1970 producer Steve Verroca, who had brought the hit single 'Volare' to the States years before, heard some of these tapes and started helping produce an album of Link's music down at the Shack.

About six months later the album was completed and Verroca started looking around for a label to release it. George Harrison was keen to put it out on Apple, but Verroca finally made a deal with Polydor, on which label it has now been released: Polydor 2489 029. And it's very tasty.

BRITISH RELEASES TO 1960
Singles
June 58   'Rumble', 'The Swag'
           London 45HLA 8623

Link Wray

BRITISH FRINGE

As well as those who developed into major disc stars, like Cliff Richard, Tommy Steele, Billy Fury and Marty Wilde, there were during the late 50's many other British performers who broke into, or at any rate were launched directly at, the rapidly expanding market for young rock and rollers. Actually, there were very few of them who could really be classified as real rockers. Their voices were too gentle, their style often too polite and inhibited, and the musicians, arrangers and managers with whom they worked were usually older men with no feel for rock. They either mechanically reproduced the music with bland professionalism, or else tried to steer the singer as rapidly as possible into the ghastly role of 'all-round family entertainer'.

Most of these artists found their brief spell of fame on television, I.T.V. in particular had a fairly generous allotment of 'young' music programmes in those days, or as supporting-bill artists on shows and tours headlined by American visitors. Their records were almost invariably cover versions of current American hits, and because of this were occasionally chart hits, the point being that the original and cover versions often sounded almost identical on the radio, and the Britisher would have the advantage of being able to promote his disc, either in concert or on T.V.

Terry Dene was a T.V. success who managed a couple of hit discs as well. He had started singing as a dance band vocalist around the South London area where he was born, but with the advent of 'Six-Five Special' moved on to rock-style solo work and became a regular performer on the show. A Decca recording contract followed, and Terry cut his first disc, a cover version of Marty Robbins' huge U.S. country-pop hit 'A White Sports Coat'. Despite stiff opposition from a third version of the song by the King Brothers, who made the Top 10 with it, Terry's T.V. plugs pushed his version to No. 18 slot in the charts. He followed up by covering Sal Mineo's 'Start Movin'', and this was a similar success, reaching No. 15 in August 1957. A part in 'The Golden Disc', a typically unreal film about the British rock music world, followed, but while he was filming Terry's disc sales slumped;

even 'The Golden Age', taken from the film to promote it, caused only minor interest. He looked around for more American material, and came up with another Marty Robbins hit in 'Stairway Of Love'. Unfortunately, it was also found by Michael Holliday, who had just soared to popularity with 'The Story Of My Life', another Robbins' pinch, and it was the Holliday version which made the Top 5. Terry's recording peaked at No. 16, and was his chart swansong. Within a couple of years, fading support, an unsuccessful marriage with Edna Savage, and finally a brief and shattering encounter with National Service, had all but finished his career. Dene vanished into obscurity, to reappear several years later as a religious crusader. Few others even managed to equal Dene's run of success. *Wee Willie Harris*, another 'Six-Five Special' regular, and the Jimmy Savile of

his day, dying his hair outrageous colours, and having a penchant for garish and outlandish clothes, also recorded for Decca, but without much success. He at least put some of the energy of genuine rock into his performances, being a piano-hammerer in the Jerry Lee Lewis/Little Richard tradition, but his appeal was that of a T.V. gimmick rather than a disc-selling teenage attraction. His records too were chiefly cover versions, 'Back To School Again', (Timmie Rogers), 'No Chemise Please', (Gerry Granahan), etc., but they didn't make the charts.

Further down amongst the also-rans were a quartet of highly unlikely names, in the form of *Vince Eager, Dickie Pride, Johnny Gentle* and *Duffy Power*. The names, and to a large extent the singers, were all manufactured by British manager/impresario Larry Parnes, who had a thing about surnaming his artists after various aspects of the human personality; Billy Fury and Marty Wilde were also products of this unique vision. They all did fairly well on the scream circuit, and all recorded: unsuccessfully. Eager, in particular, did well on T.V. where he came to be a regular performer on several shows, and his discs for Top Rank were also probably the most popular; cover versions of Floyd Robinson's 'Makin' Love', Marty Robbins' 'El Paso', Conway Twitty's 'Lonely Blue Boy', and Gene Pitney's 'Love My Life Away'. The most talented of the bunch, however, was Duffy Power, who achieved little during his rock years but went into semi-retirement to study the roots of the music and R&B styles, emerging again strongly in the

British R&B boom of the mid-60's. He made a tremendous version of 'It Ain't Necessarily So' for Parlophone in 1963, which showed just how good a vocal performer he really was, and has recently released an album.

Other minor British rockers and fringe-rockers were *Don Lang*, who with his Frantic Five was Britain's answer to Bill Haley & The Comets, and who had two hits in 'Cloudburst' and 'Witch Doctor'; *Jackie Dennis*, who scored with a cover of Billie & Lillie's 'La De Dah', and was forever on T.V.; *Laurie London*, another T.V. fixture with a U.S. million-seller in 'He's Got The Whole World In His Hands'; *Lance Fortune*; *Jim Dale*, who graduated to comedy acting; *Garry Mills*; *Lord Rockingham*; and *Joe Brown*, who became a bigger success when he expanded his talents into a pop/comedy/showbiz bag in the 1960's.

TERRY DENE RELEASES TO 1960

+British Top 20 Hit

Singles

1957 'A White Sport Coat', 'The Man In The Phone Booth' Decca 45F10895+

1957 'Green Corn', 'Start Movin'' Decca 45F10914+

1957 'Come And Get It', 'Teenage Dream' Decca 45F10938

1957 'Baby She's Gone', 'Lucky Lucky Bobby' Decca 45F10964

1957 'C'min And Be Loved', 'The Golden Age' Decca 45F10977

1958 'Lover Lover', 'Stairway Of Love' Decca 45F11016+

1958 'Can I Walk You Home', 'Seven Steps To Love' Decca 45F11037

1958 'Pretty Little Pearly', 'Who Baby Who' Decca 45F11076

1958 'Bimbombey', 'I've Got A Good Thing Going' Decca 45F11100

1959 'I've Come Of Age', 'There's No Fool Like A Young Fool' Decca 45F11136

1959 'A Boy Without A Girl', 'Thank You Pretty Baby' Decca 45F11154

1960 'Geraldine', 'Love Me Or Leave Me' Oriole 45CB1562

1960 'Like A Baby', 'Next Stop Paradise' Oriole 45CB1594

EPs

1959 'Lover Lover', 'Market Place', 'Lucky Lucky Bobby', 'This Is The Night'. Decca 6507

1959 'C'min And Be Loved', 'The Golden Age', 'Charm', 'Candy Floss' Decca 6459

The song 'This Is The Night' is included on the compilation LP 'Stars Of Six-Five Special'

Terry Dene 1958

VINCE EAGER
BRITISH RELEASES TO 1960
Singles

1959 'Five Days Five Days', 'No More' Parlophone 45R4482

1959 'The Railroad Song', 'When's Your Birthday Baby' Parlophone 45R4531

1959 'No Other Arms No Other Lips', 'This Should Go On For Ever' Parlophone 45R4550

1959 'Makin' Love', 'Primrose Love' Top Rank 45JAR191

1959 'El Paso', 'Why' Top Rank 45JAR275

1959 'Lonely Boy Blue', 'No Love Have I'. Top Rank 45JAR307

1960 'I Know What I Want', 'I Wanna Love My Life Away' Top Rank 45JAR539

EPs

1958 'Yea Yea', 'Lend Me Your Comb', 'Gum Drop', 'Soda-Pop Pop', 'Tread Softly Stranger' Decca 6504

Vince Eager in a BBC studio 1958

WEE WILLIE HARRIS
BRITISH RELEASES TO 1960
Singles

1957 'Back To School Again', 'Rockin' At the Two I's' Decca 45F10970

1957 'Love Bug Crawl', 'Rosie Lee' Decca 45F10980

1958 'Got A Match', 'No Chemise Please' Decca 45F1104

1960 'Little Bitty Girl', 'Wild One'. Decca 45F11217

EPs

1958 'Rockin' With Wee Willie': 'Rockin' At The Two Is', 'Love Bug Crawl', 'Riot In Cell Block Number Nine', 'Back To School Again' Decca 6465

LPs

No LPs, but included on the LP 'Stars Of Six-Five Special', Decca LF 1299, with the song 'Smack Dab In The Middle'.

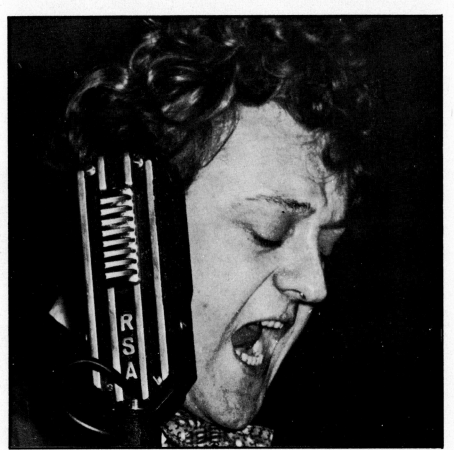

Wee Willie Harris on stage 1957

JOHNNY GENTLE BRITISH RELEASES TO 1960

Singles

1959 'Boys And Girls Were Meant For Each Other', 'Wendy' Philips 45PB908

1959 'I Like The Way', 'Milk From The Coconut' Philips 45PB945

1959 'Darlin' Won't You Wait', 'This Friendly World' Philips 45PB988

1960 'After My Laughter Came Tears', 'Sonja' Philips 45PB1069

EPs

1960 'The Gentle Touch': 'Milk From The Coconut', 'I Like The Way', 'Darlin' Won't You Wait', 'This Friendly World' Philips 12345

Johnny Gentle 1958

DUFFY POWER BRITISH RELEASES TO 1960

Singles

1959 'Dream Lover', 'That's My Little Susie' Philips 45PB927

1959 'Ain't She Sweet', 'Kissin' Time' Fontana 45H214

1959 'Prettier Than You', 'Starry Eyed' Fontana 45H230

1960 'If I Can Dream', 'Whole Lotta Shakin' Goin' On' Fontana 45H279

DICKIE PRIDE BRITISH RELEASES TO 1960

Singles

1959 'Don't Make Me Love You', 'Slippin' And Slidin'' Columbia 45DB4283

1959 'Fabulous Cure', 'Midnight Oil' Columbia 45DB4296

1959 'Franatic', 'Primrose Lane' Columbia 45DB4340

1959 'Betty Betty Go Steady With Me', 'No John' Columbia 45DB4403

1960 'Bye Bye Blackbird', 'You're Singing Our Love Song To Somebody Else' Columbia 45DB4451

EPs

1959 'The Sheik Of Shake': 'Fabulous Cure', 'Slippin' And Slidin'', 'Don't Make Me Love You', 'Midnight Oil' Columbia 7937

LPs

1960 'Pride Without Prejudice': 'Anything Goes', 'It's Only A Paper Moon', 'Isn't This A Lovely Day', 'I Could Write A Book', 'You Turned The Tables On Me', 'Too Close For Comfort', 'Loch Lomond', 'Lulu's Back In Town', 'There's A Small Hotel', 'Falling In Love', 'They Can't Take That Away From Me', 'Give Me The Simple Life' Columbia 33SX1307

Duffy Power 1958

COMPILATION RECORDS

BRITISH RELEASES TO 1960
1956
'Rock And Roll': Chuz Alfred Combo: 'Rockin' Boy', Hal Singer Band: 'Hot Rod', Bobby Banks Orchestra: 'Blues For Everybody', Rockin' Brothers Orchestra: 'Playboy Hop'; 'The Grinder', Bob Oakes Orchestra: 'You Gotta Rock An' Roll', T.J. Fowler Orchestra: 'Back Biter'; 'Wine Cooler', Paul Williams Orchestra: 'Rooser Boogie', Hal Singer Orchestra: 'Frog Hop' London HBC1067

'Rock N Roll Party': Red Prysock: 'Rock And Roll Party', 'Finger Tips', Eddie Bond And The Stompers: 'Rockin' Daddy'; 'I've Got A Woman', Ella Johnson: 'What A Day'; 'That's What You Gotta Do', Sil Austin: 'Slow Walk'; 'Wildwood', Freddie Bell and the Bellboys: 'All Right OK You Win'; 'Stay Loose Mother Goose' Mercury MPT7512

1957
'Tops In Pops No. 1.: Terry Dene: 'A White Sport Coat', Bob Cort Skiffle: 'Six Five Special', Beverley Sisters: 'Bye Bye Love', Tommy Steele: 'Butterfingers' Decca 6411
'All Star Hit Parade No. 2': Beverley Sisters: 'Freight Train', Tommy Steele: 'Butterfly', Max Bygraves: 'White Sport Coat', Billy Cotton Band: 'Puttin' On The Style', Johnston Brothers: 'Around The World', Jimmy Young: 'When I Fall In Love' Decca F10915
'Music For The Boyfriend: He Digs Rock And Roll': Bill Haley Comets: 'See You Later Alligator'; 'R-o-c-k'; 'The Saints Rock And Roll'; 'Burn That Candle', Gloria Mann: 'Partners For Life'; 'Why Do Fools Rush In', Mello-Tones: 'I'm Gonna Get'; 'I'm Just Another One In Love With You', Mel Williams: 'Roses Never Fade'; 'You're Alright Baby', Barons: 'Exactly Like You'; 'A Year And A Day' Brunswick LAT8201
'Stars Of Six Five Special': Tommy Steele: 'Swallow'; 'Singing The Blues', Lonnie Donegan: 'Diggin' My Potatoes', Chris Barber Jazz Band: 'I Never Knew Just What A Girl Could Do', Terry Dene: 'This Is The Night',

Bob Cort Skiffle: 'Six Five Special', Wee Willie Harris: 'Smack Dab In The Middle', George Melly: 'This Train', The Worried Men: 'Fraulien' Decca LF1299
Wee Willie Harris: 'Rockin' At The Two Is'; 'Back To School Again', Beryl Wayne: 'The Gipsy In My Soul', The Blue Jeans: 'Lonesome Traveller'; 'When I Get To Glory', Graham Steward Seven: 'Black Bottom Stomp'; 'When I Get To Swannee', The Worried Men: 'Nine Hundred Miles From Home': 'This Little Light', Johnny Grant: 'All Of Me' Decca LF1300
'Rock And Roll Dance Party': Alan Freed Rock And Roll Band: 'Swell'; 'Sometimes I'm Happy'; 'John Thompson'; 'Twenty One'; 'Sure'; 'Sentimental Journey'; 'Easy Rock'; 'Stop Look And Run', Jimmy Cavello House Rockers: 'Let 'Em Roll'; 'I'm With You'; 'Ooh Wee'; 'Foot Stompin'' Vogue Coral LVA 9066
'Teenage Rock': Red Prysock: 'Teenage Rock', Rusty Draper: 'Seven Come Eleven', Chuck Miller: 'Bye Bye Love', Crew Cuts: 'Susie Q' Mercury 9522
'Six Five Special': Don Lang And His Frantic Five: 'Six Five Special'; 'Ramshackle Daddy'; 'You Started Something', John Barry And The Seven: 'Let's Have

A Wonderful Time'; 'Rock A Billy Boogie'; 'Every Which Way', Terry Wayne: 'Boppin' The Blues'; 'Teenage Boogie', Jim Dale: 'Crazy Dream'; 'Just Born', King Brothers: 'Coldcold Shower'; 'Party Time', Laurie London: 'Pick A Bale Of Cotton'; 'Up Above My Head I Hear Music In The Air'. Jimmy Jackson: 'Six Five Jive' Parlophone PMC1047
'London Hit Parade No. 2': Fats Domino: 'Blueberry Hill', Slim Whitman: 'I'll Take You Home Again Kathleen', Ken Copeland: 'Pledge Of Love', Roy Brown: 'Saturday Night' London 1096
'Rock And Roll': Leroies Rock And Roll Band: 'Rock n Roll Bells', Mr. Goggle Eyes August: 'Oh Ho Doodle Lou', Big Walter Price Rock And Roll Band: 'Pack Fair And Square', Gatemouth Rock And Roll Band: 'Ain't That Dandy Rock' Vogue 170111
1958
'Teenage Rock': Gene Vincent: 'Dance To The Bop': Be Bop A Lula'; 'Lotta Lovin''; 'Well I Knocked And Knocked', Fremlin Husky: 'What'cha Doing After School'; 'Wang Dang Doo', Tommy Sands: 'Hep Dee Hootie'; 'Can't Change My Love'; 'Teenage Crush', Sonny James: 'Why Can't They Remember'; 'Uh-Huh-Mm' Capitol T1009
1959
'Tops In The Pops No. 7': Lord Rockingham XI: 'Wee Tom', Tommy Steele: 'Hiawatha', Beverley Sisters: 'Little Drummer Boy', Ted Heath: 'Topsy' Decca 6583
'Rockin' Together': The Coasters: 'Yakety Yak'; 'Searchin'', King Curtis: 'Ific', Bobby Darin: 'Early In The Morning'; 'Splish Splash', Jesse Stone: 'Nightlife', The Sensations: 'Yes Sir That's My Baby', Hutch Davie: 'At The

Woodchoppers Ball', Guitar Slim: 'If I Had My Life To Live Over'; 'It Hurts To Love Someone', Gerry Graham: 'Confess It To Your Heart', The Chordcats: 'Sh-Boom' London HAE2167
'Rock And Roll For Ever': Chuck Willis: 'See See Rider'; 'What Am I Living For', Ray Charles: 'Swannee River'; 'Yes Indeed', Bobettes: 'Mister Lee', Joe Turner: 'Wee Baby Blues', Clyde McPhatter: 'Come What May', LaVern Baker: 'Substitute'; 'Learnin' To Love', Ruth Brown: 'Lucky Lips', Ivory Joe Hunter: 'Empty Arms', Clovers: 'Wishing For Your Love', Drifters: 'Moonlight Bay', Jaye Sisters: 'Goin' To The River' London HAE2180
'Drumbeat': tracks by the John Barry Seven, Vince Eager, Adam Faith, Kingpins, Bob Miller And The Millermen, The Raindrops, Sylvia Sands, Roy Young and Dennis Lotis Parlophone PMC1101
'BBCTV Drumbeat': Roy Young: 'She Said Yeah', Bob Miller Millermen: 'Little Dipper'; 'Drumbeat', Sylvia Sands: 'Love Me In The Daytime', Adam Faith: 'I Vibrate', Lana Sisters: 'Buzzin' Fontana 17146
'Rushin' For Percussion': Preston Epps: 'Bongo Party'; 'Bongo Rock', Sandy Nelson: 'Teenbeat'; 'Big Jump' Top Rank 2060
'Saturday Club': Johnny Angel: 'For A Little Girl'; 'Pardon Me', John Barry Seven: 'Saturday's Child', Tommy Bruce: 'On The Sunny Side Of The Street', Danny Davis: 'Saturday Date': 'Take These Chains From My Heart', Colin Day: 'Is There Any Change', Keith Kelly: 'I'll Take Romance'; 'To Be With You', Johnny Kidd: 'Big Blon' Baby', 'Weep No More

My Baby', King Brothers: 'Five Foot Two', 'Jambalay', Ricky Valance: 'Jimmy's Girl'; 'Say Hello', Bert Weedon: 'The Creep', 'The Prowler', Garry Mills: 'Don't Forget'; 'You Alone', Tony Osborne Jazz Group: 'Saturday Jump', Sylvia Sands: 'I'm Beginning To See The Light', 'My Funny Valentine' Parlophone PMC1130
'Beat Girl Soundtrack': Adam Faith, Shirley Anne Field, and The John Barry Orchestra: 'Beat Girl', 'The Off Beat', 'I Did What You Told Me', 'Lindon Home Rock', 'Time Out', 'The Sharks', 'The Beat Girl Song', 'The City 2000AD', 'The Stripper', 'The Cave', 'Kids Stuff', 'Made You', 'Car Chase', 'Night Chase', 'Chicken', 'Blues For Beatniks', 'It's Legal', 'The Immediate Pleasure', 'Blondie's Strip', 'Slaughter In Soho' Columbia 33SX1225.

THE IMPACT ON BRITAIN

1956

May: Asa Carter of the North Alabama White Citizens Council says rock and roll 'is a means of pulling down the white man to the level of the negro. It is part of a plot to undermine the morals of the youth of our nation. It is sexualistic, unmoralistic and the best way to bring peoples of both races together'.

April: In the States Elvis is number one with 'Heartbreak Hotel', and back in rocking Britain Ted Heath is No. 2 with 'Rock and Roll Waltz'. Astute dance band leaders are not letting their (a) loathing or (b) middle age, stop them from cashing in on the rock and roll 'craze'.

June: Chuck Berry's first British release, 'No Money Down', makes a small stir in the charts. Melody Maker says 'it's raw stuff, but it goes with a swing'.

The Miami Board of Review, censors, swears to wage a fight against 'this worm wiggle' after a 10,000 crowd dances in the aisles at a Haley concert in the city.

American guitarist Bill Diehl describes Elvis as 'nothing more than a male burlesque dancer'.

July: Record sales are soaring in Britain and Rock and Roll clubs are opening up all over the country. The first is at the Oakwood Sports and Social Club, which starts to promote regular rock and roll dances.

At its European premiere at the Carlton Theatre Dublin, 'Rock Around The Clock' beats all previous attendance records.

Drummer Eric Delaney announces that he is soon to lead Britain's first 'rock and roll' band.

August: Another jazz/dance band musician, Tony Crombie, forms a 'rock and roll' band, The Rockets. Also a dance team 'to demonstrate rock and roll dancing'.

Britain's oldest modern jazz club, Vi Hylands Studio 51, closes and re-opens as the 51 Club, with a new policy of featuring trad and rock and roll bands.

Alan Freed's lawyer, Warren Throob, comes to London to negotiate a Rock and Roll Show at the Royal Albert Hall. It never happens.

September: 'Rock and Roll riots don't scare Haley' is the headline of the first lead article the Melody Maker has devoted to rock and roll. Bill Haley is due to tour Britain in February 1957.

In Blackburn the Watch Committee bans 'Rock Around The Clock', and all over the country there are similar scenes: in Preston the Chief Constable warns cinemas not to show the film. In Croydon the police try to stop people jiving in the aisles during a showing of the film. So starts the long and acrimonious association between the forces of law and order and the new music.

For the first time a jazz festival, at Butlins, Clacton, features a rock and roll group, the Kirchins. Their current disc is 'Rock and Rolling At the Darktown Strutters Ball'.

Similar pathetic attempts to cash in on rock and roll are being made by other jazz/dance musicians. Art Baxter, former vocalist with the Ronnie Scott band is fronting a rock and roll band called the Rockin' Sinners. Their first disc is 'Shortnin' Bread Rock'.

October: In Paris the police get a private preview of 'Rock Around The Clock'. Their verdict: 'Not likely to cause riots'. The next year they were to be proved massively wrong.

Bill Haley tells his story in the People.

The Carfax Assembly Rooms in Oxford starts a regular Wednesday rock and roll night. (In the early sixties the Carfax was to be one of the few funky ballrooms in the Midlands.)

November: Britain's first rock and roll movie: the outside film unit of Star Cinemas make a low budget film of a Yeadon, Yorkshire band led by Jackie Thorpe. It is called 'Rock and Roll'.

Promoter Jeff Kruger announces a plan to put on 200 rock and roll bands at a weekend festival at Brighton. Proceeds, says Kruger, are to go towards helping relief work in Hungary following the Soviet repression of the Hungarian revolt.

London's first large rock and roll jamboree is held at Wimbledon Palais. Bands featured are Rory Blackwells Rock and Rollers, Leon Bell's Bellcats, The Rock And Roll Allstars, House Rockers, and Oscars Hot Icebergs.

Jazzer Lionel Hampton is on tour in Britain, and is featuring rock and roll in his act. At his Royal Festival Hall concert Johnny Dankworth shouts out during a lull in the noise 'What about playing some jazz?'. Dankworth later said he made his protest after watching Hampton 'throwing his sticks in the air and pretending not to catch them during a drum solo'.

Worthing Corporation lifts its ban on jiving at its Civic Dances, and announces, not surprisingly, that attendances have risen.

Following his outburst at the Hampton concert Johnny Dankworth explains to the press 'All over the world wrongs are being done today. There are those who stand by and say nothing. And there are those who oppose those wrongs by the most vigorous means in their power. Thank God I'm one of the latter'. Dankworth was one of the few British bandleaders who didn't jump on the rock and roll bandwagon. December: A planned tour of Britain by Elvis is postponed due to 'Pressure of work' in the States.

Cuddly Pat Boone comes over and gives concerts at the Kilburn State and the Granada Tooting.

New star Tommy Steele gets £200, considered a huge fee, for appearing at a debs dance at Claridges. Ten weeks before he was discovered singing in a Soho coffee bar.

In order for American artists to appear in Britain the Musicians Union has insisted that a British artist must tour the States in exchange. It is announced that in exchange for Haley coming to Britain the Americans are to get Lonnie Donegan.

Rock and roll promoter Jeff Kruger said 'BBC and ITV can't see further than the end of their noses. Rock and roll has an enormous following over here but neither will give it a showing. They are just a bunch of stuffed shirts. They and the cinema managers who are scared of the name are not giving the music a fair deal.'

Not everybody could afford drapes, Banbury 1956

Leeds Locarno starts lunchtime rock and roll sessions. Admission is 3d.

The 21 year old Earl of Whancliffe, Yorks, joins the Musicians Union in order to play drums with a Sheffield rock and roll band led by Ted Pell.

Tommy Steele appears in the film 'Kill Me Tomorrow', with Pat O'Brien. 'I'm trying to get away from rock and roll now' he says. Indeed just 12 weeks after his discovery and launch as a rock artist Steele's management are already grooming him for the Variety circuit, a pattern that is to be repeated with virtually every British act up until the coming of the Beatles and the Stones in the early sixties.

According to Melody Maker the top British discs of 1956 are: 1. 'I'll Be Home' : Pat Boone; 2. 'Whatever Will Be Will Be': Doris Day; 3. 'Heartbreak Hotel' : Elvis; 4. 'A Woman in Love' : Frankie Laine; 5. 'Rockin' Through The Rye' : Bill Haley; 6. 'Why Do Fools Fall In Love' : The Teenagers; 7. 'A Tear Fell' : Teresa Brewer; 8. 'Houndog' : Elvis; 9. 'No Other Love' : Ronnie Hilton; 10. 'Rock And Roll Waltz' : Kay Starr.

1957
January: The Bill Haley tour dates are finalised and fans stampede the box offices. He is to appear at the Dominion Tottenham Court Road, February 6–9; Gaumont Coventry, 10; Odeon Nottingham, 11; Odeon Birmingham, 12; Odeon Manchester, 13; Odeon Leeds, 14; Odeon Sunderland, 15; Odeon Newcastle, 16; Gaumont Bradford, 17; Odeon Bradford, 18 and 19; Odeon Liverpool, 20; Capitol Cardiff, 21; Odeon Plymouth, 22; Gaumont Southampton, 23.

Fats Domino film 'Shake Rattle and R-o-c-k' is released.

The Elvis tour is on again.

BBCTV announce the artists to appear in its 'British Popular Song Show'. Marion Ryan, David Hughes, Lita Roza, Dennis Lotis, Eric Robinson's Concert Orchestra, Bill McGuffie Quartet and the Keynotes. There's not a rock and roll band at all, for the BBC still believe they should give the public what they ought to want rather than what they want.

The movie 'The Girl Can't

Bill Haley and Fans aboard the Bill Haley Express, Southampton to London '57

Help It' is released.

The Bill Haley tour starts, and there are no riots, although this is rectified later in the month. Further appearances are added to the already grueling schedule;: Regal Edmonton, March 3rd; Davis Theatre Croydon, 4 and 5; Carlton Cinema Norwich, 6; Gaumont Doncaster, 7; Gaumont Wolverhampton, 8; Gaumont Cheltenham, 9; Haley is also to appear at the Theatre Royal Dublin, February 27 and 28, and the Belfast Hippodrome, March 1 and 2.

BBC starts its weekly show 'Six Five Special'.

Britain's first full length rock and roll film is completed. It is called 'Rock You Sinners' and is produced by Small Films. The film features Tony Crombie and his Rockets, Art Baxter's Rockin' Sinners, Rory Blackwell's

Blackjacks, Don Sollash and his Rockin' Horses, Joan Small, George Brown and Dickie Bennett.

March: The Platters arrive for a short tour. 'We are not a rock and roll band' they say 'and do not sing rock and roll'. The group is backed by the Vic Lewis Orchestra. While in Britain they record four half hour shows for the BBC radio.

Frankie Lymon and the Teenagers arrive for a tour.

April: New British discovery Terry Dene appears on 'Six Five Special'.

May: The Platters appear on Sunday Night at the London Palladium.

An Alan Freed rock and roll show is planned to tour; likely stars are said to be Chuck Berry, Lavern Baker, The Clovers, Clyde McPhatter, Jim Bowen, Buddy

Knox, and Stan 'The Man' Taylor's band.

July: Terry Dene's disc 'Lucky Lucky Bobby' is released in the States, a courageous but ineffective move.

August: Hoaxers book several Scottish theatres for concerts by Elvis.

Tommy Steele inspired Peter Sellers pop star 'Mr. Iron' who 'doesn't want to bite the fretboard that fed me' but finds a guitar 'hanging around my neck' is hindering his efforts to get into show business proper.

Rock for the Mayfair Johnnies, the Cafe de Paris starts regular Friday night 'Rock and Roll Night'. There are no riots.

September: Tommy Steele tours Sweden, and using rock material. You see, the plan is to get first impact with rock and roll and then drop it quick and get in with

A typical audience at the BBC's 6.5 Special

the quality stuff.

The Alan Freed show, if it comes over, will feature Paul Anka, the Everly Brothers, and Little Richard in addition to the acts already announced.

Ads appear in the music press for a guitar amp called the Watkins Westminster. According to the ads the amp 'packs a ten watt punch'.

November: Terry Dene goes to South Africa on tour. On his return he suffers a nervous breakdown.

December: Tommy Steele's young brother, Colin Hicks, is launched as a rock singer. At his variety debut the audience pelt him with rotten fruit, small change and ice cream.

Paul Anka arrives for a tour.

1958

January: A Six Five Special Roadshow is put on the road, opening at the Salisbury Gaumont. Featured acts are Don Lang and his Frantic Five, Kenny Baker's Half Dozen, Jimmy Jackson Skiffle Group, Wee Willie Harris, Rosemary Squires, Carl Barriteau, Joe 'Mr. Piano' Henderson, and the Blue Star Five.

Parlophone issue a 12" Six Five Special LP; Terry Wayne, Jim Dale, King Brothers, Laurie London, Don Lang and his Frantic Five, and the Jimmy Jackson Group.

Decca issue a 10" LP called 'Stars From Six Five Special': Tommy Steele, Lonnie Donegan, Bob Cort, Wee Willie Harris, George Melly, Terry Dene, Chris Barber, and the Worried Men.

Beaconsfield Studios are making a film based on 'Six Five Special'.

'Heartbreak Hotel' is played on the daily radio programme 'Lift Up Your Hearts'. Quite a breakthrough.

Terry Dene is fined for being drunk and disorderly: 'In future it's soft drinks for me' he says.

February: Marty Wilde is the new British sensation.

Wilde makes nine TV appearances in five days, appearing on 'Six Five Special', 'Top Numbers', 'The Jack Jackson Show' and 'Cool For Cats', among other shows.

March: Buddy Holly and the Crickets arrive for a tour. Their first date is at the Trocadero, Elephant and Castle on 2nd March, and they appear on Sunday Night at the London Palladium the next day. A further couple of dozen appearances are made round the country and support acts are Gary Miller and the Tanner Sisters.

Terry Dene suffers another nervous breakdown and cancels all his scheduled gigs.

Tommy Steele goes off on a South African tour despite efforts by the Afrikaaner newspaper 'Die Vaterland' to stop the tour. A concert in Pretoria is banned for being 'prejudicial to public morals'.

Paul Anka is back for another short tour, backed by the Vic Hammet Orchestra. Support acts are Lorrae Desmond and the Fentones.

The Terry Dene film 'Gold Disc' is premiered at the Rialto West End, while Dene is a voluntary patient in hospital.

Alan Freed is 'still hoping' to bring his show over.

April: Wee Willie Harris, 27, is fined £5 for driving a car with inefficient brakes at Otley Magistrates' Court.

Tommy Steele is waxed by Madame Tussauds.

Terry Dene's agent, Hymie

Don Lang and his Frantic Five, 6.5 Special regulars

Zahl, has 'big plans' for Dene. 'Provided he behaves himself. I can't stand any more nonsense'. Dene starts ten week tour.

May: Jerry Lee Lewis arrives for British tour.

Terry Dene receives his call-up papers.

Jerry Lee has to cut short his tour because of a nasty furore over his 13 year old wife. Promoter Leslie Grade, who was instrumental in getting the tour stopped, said 'If he had gone on it might have done irreparable harm to British show business and pop music in general.'

July: Marty Wilde appears on Ed Sullivan's 'Toast of the Town' TV show from the Brussels World Fair.

Terry Dene weds Edna Savage. Their debut as a double act is at the Chiswick Empire.

August: Marty Wilde sacks the Wildcats and signs the John Barry Seven. The Wildcats were Ken Orpen and Kenny Packwood on guitars, Bert Lankester on bass and Jack Potter on drums. Wilde's manager Larry Parnes says he needed a bigger band behind him.

Wee Willie Harris has his face cut by flying pennies thrown during a concert in Oxford Town Hall. He had to leave the stage after three numbers.

ITV launch 'Oh Boy', produced by Jack Good, as their answer, a very good one, to BBC's 'Six Five Special'. Marty Wilde is featured most weeks.

September: Elvis, in Germany, plans a three day private visit to the U.K.

October: Presley visit off.

Manager Larry Parnes pulls Marty Wilde out of 'Oh Boy' because Cliff Richard is appearing too.

November: 'Hoots Mon' by Lord Rockinghams XI, the house band

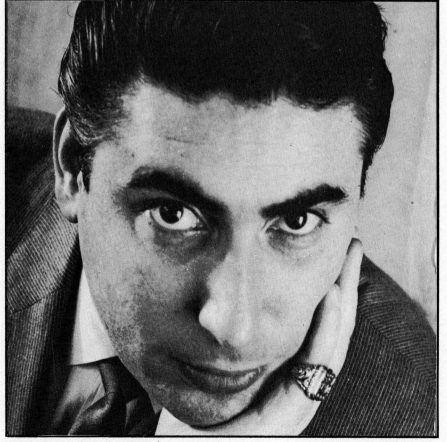

Larry Parnes, Jack Good (top)

96

on 'Oh Boy', is No. 1.

West Side Story opens in London.

December: Cliff's dad fires Cliff's personal manager Franklyn Boyd. Agent George Ganjou continues as Cliff's sole management. Says Boyd, 'We've been personal friends, I can't understand it'.

1959
January: An 'Oh Boy' stage show starts a week at the Commodore Theatre in Hammersmith. Acts are Cliff Richard, Lord Rockinghams XI, Vince Taylor, Neville Taylor and the Cutters, the Dallas Boys Cherry Wainer, Peter Elliot and Cuddly Duddly.

Larry Parnes and Jack Goode make it up; Marty Wilde is back on 'Oh Boy' for six shows as soon as he finishes his booking in the Robin Hood panto at the Hippodrome Stockton.

'Hoots Mon' has sold 600,000.

The Everly Brothers, the Chordettes and Andy Williams arrive in the U.K. for the start of a TV promotional tour taking in eight European countries.

Harry Robinson, leader of Lord Rockinghams XI, takes Jack Good to court over the rights to the name 'Lord Rockinghams XI'.

March: Elvis may holiday in Britain!

Harry Robinson withdraws the action against Good and admits that Good holds copyright to the name. As a result Robinson resumes his position as bandleader on 'Oh Boy'.

EMI stops making 78 rpm records.

April: Larry Parnes is now *the* British rock and roll manager. Six of his boys are appearing on 'Oh Boy' and BBC's rival 'Drumbeat' this month: Marty Wilde, Dickie Pride, Billy Fury, Vince Eager,

Duffy Power and Johnny Gentle.

Marty Wilde attacks session men: at a concert in Bradford he tells the audience, 'In the past my record backings have been corny and square and the kids can spot them a mile off. Philips wouldn't let the Wildcats back me. I fought for a year and a week ago they agreed to let them back me on fast rocking numbers. It takes youngsters to play and feel the rock beat.'

Jack Good signed as freelance producer to Decca.

Elvis will not holiday in Britain after all.

May: Conway Twitty flies in to star on 'Oh Boy'.

The Platters postpone their scheduled nine week Variety tour due to the sudden illness of girl singer Zola Taylor.

'Oh Boy' takes a break till September.

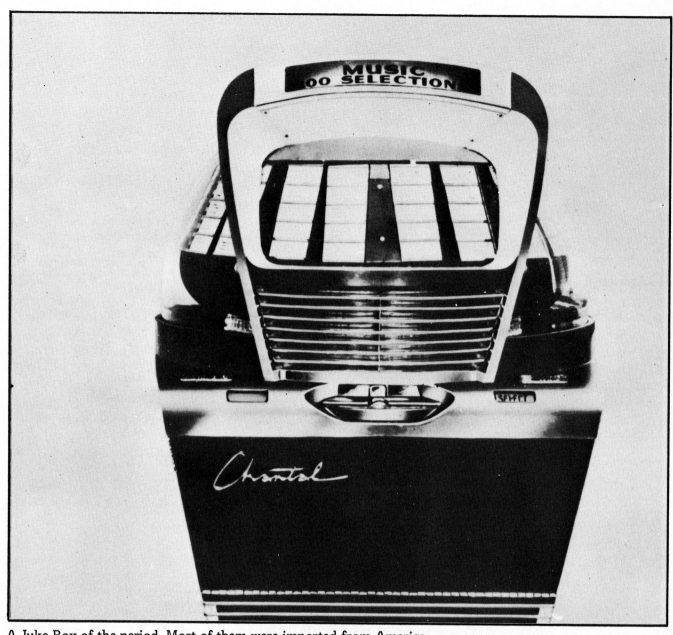

A Juke Box of the period. Most of them were imported from America

June: The BBC start Juke Box Jury.

August: After only a short time, the BBC kill 'Drumbeat'. Regulars on the programme were Adam Faith, Vince Eager, John Barry, Bob Miller's Millermen, Sylvia Sands and Danny Williams.

Marty Wilde announces that he wants to become an allround entertainer: 'I'm approaching 21 now and think it's about time that I branched out as an allround entertainer. I want to drop most of the rock stuff and do the real class stuff like Sinatra.'

September: 'Oh Boy' returns.

November: The Grade brothers announce that the Everly Brothers will tour in early 1960.

December: Gene Vincent arrives to appear on Jack Good's 'Boy Meets Girls' ABCTV show. He appears on the December 9, 19 and 26 shows. He also does a concert at the Granada Tooting and a 3 minute interview on Saturday Club.

Vincent decides to stay in Britain till October 1960. Larry Parnes signs him to an exclusive 30 week contract.

Clyde McPhatter, Bobby Darin and Duane Eddy are fixed to tour in March 1960.

Eddie Cochran signed to appear on 'Boy Meets Girls' January 16 and 23.

ROCK 'N'ROLL MOVIES

This list covers films made 1956–1960 in the U.S.A. or U.K. which featured rock and roll music/musicians.

'Beat Girl' (Anglo Amalgamated) UK 1959
Adam Faith
John Barry Seven
'Because They're Young' (Columbia) USA 1960
Duane Eddy & The Rebels
Dick Clark
'The Big Beat' (Universal) USA 1958
Fats Domino
Charlie Barnet
Buddy Bregman
Alan Copeland
Del Vikings
The Diamonds
The Four Aces
Harry James
The Mills Brothers
The Lancers
Freddie Martin
Russ Morgan
George Shearing Quintet
Jan Southern
Bill Thompson Singers
Cal Tjader Trio
'Calypso Heat Wave' (Columbia) USA 1957
The Treniers
The Tarriers
The Hi-Los
'Disc Jockey Jamboree' (Warner Bros.) USA 1957
Jerry Lee Lewis
Fats Domino
Buddy Knox
Jimmy Bowen
Charlie Gracie
The Four Coins
Count Basie
Joe Williams
Jodie Sands
Carl Perkins
Slim Whitman
Lewis Lyman and the Teenchords

Ron Coby
Connie Francis
Andy Martin
Frankie Avalon
Rocco and his Saints
'Don't Knock The Rock' (Columbia) USA 1956
Bill Haley and the Comets
Alan Freed
The Treniers
Little Richard
Dave Appell and the Applejacks
Jovada
Jimmy Ballad
'Duke Wore Jeans' (Anglo Amalgamated) UK 1958
Tommy Steele
'The Girl Can't Help It' (20th Century Fox) USA 1957
Eddie Cochran
Tommy Ewell
Jayne Mansfield
Edmond O'Brien
Julie London
Ray Anthony
Barry Gordon
Fats Domino
The Platters
Little Richard
Gene Vincent and the Bluecaps
The Treniers
Eddie Fontaine
Chuckles
Abbey Lincoln
Johnny Olen
Nino Tempo
'Go Johnny Go' (Valiant) USA 1959
Eddie Cochran
Chuck Berry
Alan Freed
Jimmy Clanton
Sandy Stewart
Ritchie Valens
Jackie Wilson
Harvey of the Moonglows
The Cadillacs
The Flamingoes
Jo Ann Campbell

'The Golden Disc' (Associated British Pathe) UK 1958
Terry Dene
Les Hobeaux
Dennis Lotis
Nancy Whiskey
Murray Campbell
Shiela Buxton
Phil Seamen
Bonny Stewart and the Skiffle Kings
Terry Kennedy Group
'High School Confidential' (MGM) USA 1958
Jerry Lee Lewis
Ray Anthony
'Hot Rod Gang' (Anglo Amalgamated) USA 1959
Gene Vincent and the Bluecaps
'Jailhouse Rock' (MGM) USA 1957
Elvis Presley
'Juke Box Rhythm' (Columbia) USA 1959
Johnny Oris
The Nitwits
Earl Grant Trio
Jack Jones
'Kill Me Tomorrow' (Anglo Amalgamated) UK 1956
Tommy Steele
'King Creole' (Paramount) USA 1958
Elvis Presley
'Let's Rock' (Columbia) USA 1958
Paul Anka
Danny & The Juniors
Roy Hamilton
Royal Teens
Tyrones
Wink Martindale
Julia La Rosa
Della Reese
'The Lost Lagoon' (United Artists) USA 1958
Don Gibson
Roger Clark
Sammy Gary
June Hartley

Bill Haley and the Comets in Don't Knock the Rock

Little Richard and band in Don't Knock the Rock

'Love Me Tender' (20th Century Fox) USA 1956
Elvis Presley
'Loving You' (Paramount) USA 1957
Elvis Presley
'Mr. Rock & Roll' (Paramount) USA 1957
Chuck Berry
Alan Freed
Brook Benton
Teddy Randazzo
Moonglows

Clyde McPhatter
Frankie Lymon and the Teenagers
Lavern Baker
Ferlin Husky
Lionel Hampton
'Rock All Night' (Anglo Amalgamated) USA 1957
The Platters
The Blockbusters
'Rock Rock Rock' (Warners) USA 1957
Alan Freed
Chuck Berry

Frankie Lymon and the Teenagers
The Moonglows
Johnny Burnette Trio
The Flamingoes
Lavern Baker
'Rock And Roll' (Outisde film unit of Star Cinemas, Yorkshire) UK 1956
Jackie Thorpe Rock and Roll Band
'Rock Around The Clock' (Columbia) USA 1955
Bill Haley and the Comets

Jerry Lee Lewis in High School Confidential

The Platters
Tony Martinez and his Band
Freddie Bell and the Bellboys
Alan Freed
'Rock Baby, Rock It' (J.G. Tiger)
USA 1958
Johnny Caroll
Roscoe Gordon
'Rock Pretty Baby' (Universal)
USA 1960
Sal Mineo
'Rock You Sinners' (Small Films)
UK 1957

Tony Crombie and his Rockets
Art Baxters Rockin' Sinners
Rory Blackwells Blackjacks
Joan Small
Don Sollash and his Rockin'
Horses
George Brown
Dickie Bennett
'Shake Rattle and R-o-c-k'
(American-International) USA
1957
Fats Domino
Joe Turner

Tommy Charles
Choker Campbell
Anita Ray
'Sing Boy Sing'
(20th Century Fox) USA 1958
Tommy Sands
'The Tommy Steele Story'
(Anglo Amalgamated) UK 1957
Tommy Steele
'Untamed Youth'
(Warners) USA 1957
Eddie Cochran
The Hollywood Rock & Rollers

Gene Vincent and the Blue Caps in The Girl Can't Help It

Frankie Avalon in Let's Rock

The Platters in Rock Around the Clock

Fats Domino in Shake Rattle and R-o-c-k

NORMAN PETTY
TALKS ABOUT BUDDY HOLLY

Norman Petty was more than just Buddy Holly's manager, he contributed to the songwriting of many Holly hits and was closely involved with their production and arranging. This interview is extracted from a tape recorded conversation with Petty in the early 60s.

There's some dispute over who wrote 'Peggy Sue'. Who did write it?

'You'll see on the copyright that it was Norman Petty as co-writer on it and Jerry Allison. Well, this isn't so. I'll tell you what the truth is : Jerry Allison had a girl friend at the time by the name of Peggy Sue. At the time Buddy came up with a melody and brought it into the control room at 5.30 one morning and he said I think we ought to name a song after Jerry's girl friend. So in actuality Jerry came up with the title so to speak, Buddy wrote the melody and I came up with the lyrics. So from 5.30 to about 9.30 this particular morning we wrote the song and recorded it.'

Where did you record with Buddy?

'In Clovis, New Mexico the majority of them. We did record a few on the road and then of course we would take them back to New Mexico and add the echo sound there.'

'Oh Boy' was recorded on the road wasn't it?

Well this one is an interesting record because at the time that we recorded this particular number my trio was playing in Oklahoma City and Buddy was on the road and had two days off and he stopped by Oklahoma City. I carried my recording equipment with me so we recorded the major

sound track 'dry' as we'd say (without echo) in one corner of the Officers Club in Oklahoma City one night after it closed up: and then of course Buddy continued on the road.

How did Buddy come to record 'Rave On'?

It was brought to me by two fellows by the name of Sonny West and Mil Telman and they brought this thing to me as strictly a hillbilly number. I was playing the tape in the control room and Buddy came in and said I rather like that, it's a real hillbilly thing. So I said would you like to do it if we change the lyrics, so Buddy said sure. So I rewrote the lyrics and out came 'Rave On'.'

I've always wanted to know, who played sax on 'Early In The Morning'?

This was one of the few that was recorded in New York with the Orchestra under the direction of Dick Jacobs and it had Sam 'The Man' Taylor doing the wildest sax in the business . . . . . we always recorded with Buddy either late at night or early in the morning.'

What were the events leading up to the air crash?

'Well no-one knows the entire story, but there's not a great deal of mystery surrounding it. Buddy of course was on tour and as you know a lot of the artists are crowded into the buses and they have just so many hours between jobs you might say. And if there's a great deal of mileage to be covered then immediately after the show closes one night in one city they jump on the bus and go to the next. And I'm sure that Buddy was quite worried about this type of thing because it didn't

give him a chance to have clean clothes or really feel like he'd settled down in any place. So he and Richie Valens and the Big Bopper decided they'd charter this private plane so they could get into the next town early to get their laundry done and of course to get themselves some rest in a bed rather than sleeping on the bus.

'So I'm sure this is what started the whole thing. They paid for the plane, and this young pilot agreed to take them out, even though the weather didn't look too favourable. But the boys insisted and of course they did take off in this light snow storm and I feel sure the young pilot wasn't familiar with the type of aircraft he was flying : and all the time he thought he was going up he was in fact going right towards the ground.'

Were there any special career plans for Buddy at the time of his death?

'Of course Buddy had some plans of his own but the thing that was the most exciting to me was that Buddy had asked me to get in touch with Ray Charles. He wanted to do a complete album at Ray Charles' suggestion because Buddy felt that Ray Charles was one of the greatest performers that he had ever seen or had ever met. We were going to have Ray Charles do a complete album: select the musicians, select the songs, everything and Buddy would be the sort of front boy . . . . and come up with a great album.'

Was it you or Buddy who first suggested string orchestrations?

'I'd suggested we go the big orchestra string route, so that

Buddy could branch into nightclub work on his own, you know, without the rock group if rock and roll became less important. Buddy wasn't in favour of this at first and then out of the clear blue sky when we were in the airport at San Francisco he said he was keen to make some recordings with strings. Well I was quite startled, and we were going to New York and when we got there we decided on four numbers: 'It Doesn't Matter Any More', 'Moondream', 'True Love Ways', and of course 'Rainin' In My Heart', all done with the Dick Jacobs strings.'

Why did Peggy Sue get married?

'Well, I suppose because Jerry Allison proposed to her! This particular song was one Buddy had written and recorded at home on his own tape recorder and which was later added on to in the studio.

'Incidentally, this recorder was the one that all his hits were recorded on: he'd asked me to buy him a recorder so I said well it'll cost X number of dollars. He said why don't you buy the new one and give me this one. I said well this is an old one and he said I know but this is the one all my hits were recorded on.

'So he had made this tape of 'Peggy Sue Got Married' on his own and it was in his apartment at the time of his death and of course it was handed to the record company and spliced and re-spliced and then we put some backing to it in New York and it was released.'

How well did Buddy know the Everly Brothers?

'I believe he first met the boys in New York and then later on he would visit them in Nashville in their home and of course the boys

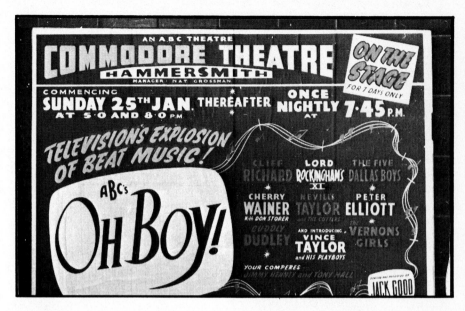

would be on tour or they would be visiting each other whenever they possibly could : whenever their careers allowed. They admired each other as artists I believe very greatly.

'Buddy certainly thought a lot of them and it's illustrated by the way he changed his dress style. The first time I saw Buddy on stage I was quite shocked. He was wearing a bright red jacket, bright red shoes and white trousers. And of course after I saw that I decided they would have to go because he was playing to some adult audiences too. Of course Buddy at first resented the idea of someone trying to tell him how to dress, but after he saw the neatness and Continental look of Phil and Don he felt that probably it wasn't such a bad idea after all.

'Love Made A Fool Of You' was originally done as a demo for the Everlys; Buddy came up with the song ideas and he wanted them to record this so he did the two vocal tracks himself and he caught a plane to Nashville and took this tape to Don and Phil and asked that they recorded it. Well of course at the time they were tied to a different publishing firm

and they said we don't want to record the song because we know you would cover us. Of course they were rising Buddy a bit and he had no intention of covering it: he did not want them to do it'.

Don Everly On Norman Petty
From an Interview in 'Zig Zag' with John Tolber

John Tobler 'We hear that Buddy Holly used to wear pink jackets and Presley type clothing and that Norman Petty and you influenced him to smarten up.'

Don Everly 'Norman Petty had no influence on him whatsoever, except that he used to put 10% of his record royalties into a Norman Petty trust fund. Someone told us about 6 months earlier that our clothes were terrible and he took us to this place to get fitted out. So we took him to the same place .... Yeah, he had some pretty awful suits that he'd had made in Lubbock, Texas. The last time I saw Buddy Holly, he'd been financially screwed, he didn't have any money, and he was on his last tour. He was killed in that plane because he was trying to gain a day for laundry and so on by flying.'

'OH BOY'

Even seen today, Jack Good's 'Oh Boy' programmes remain extremely entertaining, and contain some fine rock and roll. In 1958 and 1959 their impact was simply tremendous. For the first time in Britain here was a regular TV show featuring a high proportion of rock and roll, with no jokes and no tired comedy routines.

'Oh Boy' was made each week at the Hackney Empire before an invited audience of two hundred and fifty rock and roll fans. For their benefit the show was presented as a regular stage concert, and the cameras intruded as little as possible. As a result, the atmosphere of the show was quite unlike anything else on British TV at the time, and even in America there was nothing to compete with it. The average weekly TV audience for the show was ten million.

Back-up music was provided by the John Barry Seven and Lord Rockingham's XI, plus three vocal groups, the Dallas Boys, Neville Taylor and his Cutters, and the Vernon Girls.

When 'Oh Boy' ended in 1959, Jack Good produced another TV rock show called 'Boy Meets Girl', and went to America to produce similar shows on TV there.

'Oh Boy' was compered by Jimmy Henney, and the musical direction for most shows was Harry Robinson (otherwise known as Lord Rockingham). Dance routines were directed by Leslie Cooper and the overall director of the show was Rita Gillespie.

Cliff Richard, Oh Boy September 13 1958

The following list gives details of the cast of every 'Oh Boy' show transmitted from London. The first two shows were on Sundays from 10.50 – 11.20 p.m., and the remaining ones from 6.00 – 6.30 p.m. on Saturdays.

June 15th 1958
Marty Wilde
The Dallas Boys
John Barry Seven
Lord Rockingham's XI
Cherry Wainer and Red Price
Neville Taylor and his Cutters
The Vernon Girls
Bernice Reading
Dudley Heslop
Kerry Martin

June 29th
Marty Wilde
Bernice Reading
Ronnie Carroll
Jackie Dennis
The Dallas Boys
The John Barry Seven
Cherry Wainer and Red Price
Lord Rockingham's XI
Neville Taylor and his Cutters
The Vernon Girls

September 13th
Marty Wilde
Cliff Richard and the Drifters
Bernice Reading
Ronnie Carroll
The Dallas Boys
Cherry Wainer and Red Price
The John Barry Seven
Lord Rockingham's XI
Neville Taylor and his Cutters
The Vernon Girls

September 20th
Marty Wilde
Cliff Richard and the Drifters
Ronnie Carroll
The Dallas Boys
Cherry Wainer
The John Barry Seven
Lord Rockingham's XI
Neville Taylor and his Cutters
The Vernon Girls
Red Price
Dudley Heslop

September 27th
Marty Wilde
Ronnie Carroll
The Dallas Boys
The John Barry Seven
Neville Taylor and his Cutters
Cherry Wainer
Lone Mann
Lord Rockingham's XI
Red Price

October 4th
Marty Wilde Vince Eager
Ronnie Carroll Don Lang The
Dallas Boys
Neville Taylor and his Cutters
Cherry Wainer
Lord Rockingham's XI
The Vernon Girls
Red Price

October 11th
Marty Wilde
Cliff Richard and the Drifters
Ronnie Carroll
Valerie Shane
The Dallas Boys
Neville Taylor and his Cutters
Dudley Heslop
Cherry Wainer
Lord Rockingham's XI
The Vernon Girls
Red Price

October 18th
Marty Wilde
Cliff Richard and the Drifters
Neville Taylor and his Cutters
Cherry Wainer
The Dallas Boys
The Vernon Girls
Ronnie Carroll
Jackie Dennis
The John Barry Seven
Lord Rockingham's XI
Red Price

October 25th
Cliff Richard and the Drifters
The Dallas Boys
Neville Taylor and his Cutters
The Vernon Girls
Cherry Wainer
Peter Elliot
Red Price
Lord Rockingham's XI

November 1st
Cliff Richard
Cherry Wainer
The John Barry Seven
Peter Elliot
The Dallas Boys
Neville Taylor and his Cutters
The Vernon Girls
Dudley Heslop
Red Price
Lord Rockingham's XI
Bill Forbes

November 8th
Cliff Richard
The Dallas Boys
Peter Elliott
Neville Taylor and his Cutters
Red Price
Cherry Wainer
The Vernon Girls
Lord Rockingham's XI
Cuddly Dudley

November 15th
Cliff Richard and the Drifters
Cuddly Dudley
The Vernon Girls
Cherry Wainer
The Dallas Boys
Neville Taylor and his Cutters
The John Barry Seven
Peter Elliott
Red Price
Pat Lawrence
Lord Rockingham's XI
The Two Vernon Girls

November 22nd
Cliff Richard and the Drifters
The Dallas Boys
Neville Taylor and his Cutters
Cherry Wainer
Peter Elliott
Lord Rockingham's XI
The Vernon Girls
Red Price
Cuddly Dudley
Lone Mann

November 29th
Cliff Richard and the Drifters
The Vernon Girls
Red Price
Cherry Wainer
The Dallas Boys

Vince Eager, Oh Boy October 4 1958

Neville Taylor and his Cutters
Peter Elliott
Lord Rockingham's XI
Cuddly Dudley
Emile Ford
    December 6th
Cliff Richard and the Drifters
Michael Holliday
Cherry Wainer
Lord Rockingham's XI

Peter Elliott
The Dallas Boys
Cuddly Dudley
The John Barry Seven
Red Price
The Vernon Girls
    December 20th
Cliff Richard and the Drifters
Vince Taylor
The King Brothers

Cherry Wainer
Cuddly Dudley
Peter Elliott
Lord Rockingham's XI
The Vernon Girls
Neville Taylor and his Cutters
Red Price
The Two Vernon Girls
    January 3rd 1959
Vince Taylor and his Playboys

Cliff Richard and Marty Wilde, Oh Boy October 11 1958

Don Lang
The Dallas Boys
Cherry Wainer
Lord Rockingham's XI
Cuddly Dudley
Neville Taylor and his Cutters
The Vernon Girls
Red Price
Peter Elliott
William Marshall

January 10th
Terry Dene
Vince Taylor and his Playboys
Don Lang
Mona Baptiste
The Dallas Boys
Cherry Wainer
Lord Rockingham's XI
Peter Elliott
Cuddly Dudley

Neville Taylor and his Cutters
Red Price
The Vernon Girls
January 17th
Cliff Richard and the Drifters
Mona Baptiste
Cherry Wainer
The Dallas Boys
Peter Elliott
Neville Taylor and his Cutters

The Dallas Boys

Vince Taylor, Oh Boy January 3 1959

left to right: Peter Elliot, Mona Baptiste, Don Lang and Terry Dene
during rehearsals for Oh Boy January 10 1959

Bill Forbes
Lord Rockingham's XI
Red Price
The Vernon Girls
January 24th
Lonnie Donegan and his Skiffle
Group
Roy Young
Mike Preston
Cherry Wainer

Bill Forbes
The Hewitt Sisters
The Dallas Boys
Lord Rockingham's XI
The Vernon Girls
Red Price
Neville Taylor and his Cutters
January 31st
Cliff Richard and the Drifters
Shirley Bassey

The Dallas Boys
Don Lang
Neville Taylor and his Cutters
Cherry Wainer
Lord Rockingham's XI
The Vernon Girls
Red Price
February 7th
Marty Wilde
Cliff Richard and the Drifters

Neville Taylor and his Cutters, Oh Boy January 3 1959

Lord Rockingham's XI
Cherry Wainer
The Dallas Boys
Betty Miller
Neville Taylor and his Cutters
The Vernon Girls
Red Price
   February 14th
Marty Wilde
Billy Fury

Shirley Bassey
Lord Rockingham's XI
Cherry Wainer
Don Lang
The Mudlarks
Peter Elliott
The Dallas Boys
The Vernon Girls
Red Price
   February 21st

Marty Wilde
Don Lang
The Dallas Boys
Cherry Wainer
Lord Rockingham's XI
Betty Miller
The Vernon Girls
Red Price
Gerry Dorsey
Rikki Henderson

Billy Fury, Oh Boy February 14 1959

February 28th
Marty Wilde
Dickie Pride
Tony Sheridan
Lord Rockingham's XI
Cherry Wainer
Cuddly Dudley
Bill Forbes
The Dallas Boys
Mike Preston
Neville Taylor and his Cutters
Red Price

The Vernon Girls
March 7th
Cliff Richard and the Drifters
Marty Wilde
Vince Eager
Marion Ryan
The Dallas Boys
Cherry Wainer
Mike Preston
The Vernon Girls
Red Price
Lord Rockingham's XI

Neville Taylor and his Cutters
March 14th
Billy Fury
Tony Sheridan
Chris Andrews
Don Lang
Cherry Wainer
The Dallas Boys
Neville Taylor and his Cutters
Red Price
Bill Forbes
Peter Elliott

Tony Sheridan, Oh Boy February 18 1959. The Beatles made their
first-ever record with Sheridan in Germany a few years later.

Terry and Freddy
The Vernon Girls
March 21st
Marty Wilde
Tony Sheridan
Dickie Valentine
The Dallas Boys
Cherry Wainer
Neville Taylor and his Cutters
Cuddly Dudley
Red Price
Gerry Dorsey

The Vernon Girls
March 28th
Cliff Richard and the Drifters
The Marino Marini Quartet
Ronnie Carroll
Neville Taylor and his Cutters
Cherry Wainer
The Dallas Boys
The Vernon Girls
Red Price
Pierce Rodgers
April 4th

Dickie Pride
Tony Sheridan
Chris Andrews
Cherry Wainer
Don Lang
Lord Rockingham's XI
Neville Taylor and his Cutters
Mike Preston
Lone Mann
Red Price
The Vernon Girls
Dean Webb

The Vernon Girls

Billy Fury and Joe Brown, Boy Meets Girl 1960

Gene Vincent and Joe Brown, Boy Meets Girl 1960

April 11th
Marty Wilde
Dickie Pride
The Vernon Girls
Lord Rockingham's XI
Cuddly Dudley
Cherry Wainer
The Dallas Boys
Pierce Rodgers
Neville Taylor and his Cutters
Lone Mann
Bill Forbes
Red Price

April 18th
Lonnie Donegan
Dickie Pride
Tony Sheridan
The Inkspots
Cherry Wainer
The Vernon Girls
Neville Taylor and his Cutters
The Dallas Boys
Lone Mann
Pierce Rodgers
Red Price
Jack Good's Lord
Rockingham's XI

April 25th
Billy Fury
Dickie Pride
Don Lang
Bill Forbes
Cuddly Dudley
The Dallas Boys
The Cutters
Nicky Martyn
The Vernon Girls
Red Price
Jack Good's Lord
Rockingham's XI

May 2nd
Marty Wilde
Cliff Richard and the Drifters
Alma Cogan
The Dallas Boys
Mike Preston
Cherry Wainer
Red Price
The Vernon Girls
Lord Rockingham's XI

May 9th
Terry Dene
Conway Twitty

Marty Wilde
Billy Fury
Dickie Pride
Tony Sheridan and the Wreckers
Cherry Wainer
Cuddly Dudley
The Dallas Boys
Maureen Kershaw
The Vernon Girls
Lord Rockingham's XI
Red Price

May 16th
Conway Twitty
Marty Wilde
Don Lang
Lord Rockingham's XI
Cherry Wainer
The Dallas Boys
Bill Forbes
Mike Preston
Mike Jackson
Pierce Rodgers
The Vernon Girls
Red Price

May 23rd
Cliff Richard
Marty Wilde
Dickie Pride
Billy Fury
Renee Martez
Red Price
The Dallas Boys
Cherry Wainer
Bill Forbes
Terry White
The Vernon Girls
Lord Rockingham's XI

May 30th
Cliff Richard and the Drifters
Marty Wilde
Billy Fury
Dickie Pride
The Dallas Boys
Cherry Wainer
Lord Rockingham's XI
Don Lang
Red Price
The Vernon Girls
Neville Taylor and his Cutters
Cuddly Dudley
Mike Preston
Peter Elliott
Bill Forbes

HOW TO COLLECT ORIGINAL ROCK'N'ROLL RECORDS

Many of the records mentioned in this book are available today as re-issues, usually on album compilations. But there are just as many that only exist in their original pressings and can only be bought second-hand. This section should help you get started on a collection of these tracks.

It is worth remembering that many re-issues do not have the same degree of punch the original pressings produced; re-issues on album compilations have often been 'enhanced' with stereo, as the record companies say, and in many cases the sound that comes out of your speakers has suffered as a result. Re-issues are cheaper though. The Big Bopper's 1959 album is available on re-issues for around £1, while an original pressing (almost inevitably scratched) may cost £15.

Basically there are three sources of second-hand original pressings: Specialist Magazines, Mail Order Record Lists, and Rock and Roll Record Shops.

SPECIALIST MAGAZINES

On the specialist magazine front in England 'SMG' Publications dominate the scene with three heavily R&R slanted magazines. The main one is called 'SMG'. It is a monthly, duplicated quarto magazine with a minimum of twenty-six pages, and is very helpful to the beginner-collector. Every issue includes a look at jazz/blues/R&B/Soul, but concentrates on Rock and Roll. Unlike the majority of specialist magazines, 'SMG' devotes much of its space to facts and information about record charts of previous years, as well as charts of gold discs. The back half-dozen pages

contain lists of R&R records for sale, magazines and fan clubs.

The main regular offshoot of 'SMG' is another monthly duplicated magazine called 'HBS', which is essentially an R&B/Soul magazine, but it does infrequently feature some R&R. 'SMG' does, however, run two very informative quarterly A4 sized magazines called 'Rumble' and 'Kommotion'. The former is the only magazine in the world that is devoted entirely to R&R instrumentals. Although still in its infancy it is already becoming widely-known and the first issues are much sought after. 'Kommotion' on the other hand deals with all forms of R&R except instrumentals. The latest venture from 'SMG' was the publication of a complete listing of all the records released on the London label '8000' series. It's over forty pages long, and lists not only the releases but also their original US labels and numbers.

Apart from the 'SMG' publications there is another very worthwhile magazine called 'New Rockpile'. Run by Eddie Muir as a bi-monthly duplicated quarto magazine, 'New Rockpile' covers all aspects of R&R. Perhaps one of the nicest features is the columns devoted to British R&R groups, and the various Appreciation Societies that are springing up all over the country. The only other specialist magazine currently coming out in Britain is 'Not Fade Away', which, unlike the others mentioned above, is actually printed and not duplicated. It is bi-monthly.

Outside the UK there are many publications dealing with various aspects of the music, and one of the best is the Dutch

magazine 'Rockville International', which is a monthly printed effort twenty-four pages long, with about half of it in English. Of the other European magazines the Norwegian-produced 'Whotta Lotta Rock" is good and all the articles are in English.

In the U.S.A. 'Rolling Rock' must qualify as the top magazine. Ron Weiser, the editor, also runs his own record label with some very rare material on it. Greg Shaw's 'Who Put The Bomp' runs a close second to 'Rolling Rock'. 'Who Put The Bomp' not only covers the scene in the States but also in the UK. The outstanding features of 'Who Put The Bomp' must be the detailed rundown of every fanzine that is published. Every issue of this magazine lists a host of fanzines covering every branch of music.

ADDRESSES

'SMG'/'HBS'/'Rumble'/'London Listing' : Barry Lazell, 48, Gifford Road, Benfleet, Essex.

'Kommotion' : Pete Smart, 55, Hazlewood Road, Limpsfield Chart, Oxted, Surrey.

'New Rockpile' : Eddie Muir, 152, Upper Lewes Road, Brighton, Sussex.

'Rockville International' : Adri Sturn, Nieuwstraat 2, Vrouwenpolder, Holland.

Whole Lotta Rockin" : Rune Halland, Asv 8, 1400 Ski, Norway.

'Rollin' Rock' : Ron Weiser, 10735, Bluffside Drive, N. Hollywood, California 91604, U.S.A.

'Who Put The Bomp' : Bob Fisher, 16, Yorkshire Road, Leicester. (The English distributor).

Most of these magazines are

run on a very low budget, so include an s.a.e. when writing to them.

The fan club scene: there are very few noteworthy ones still running, but the following can provide useful information on discographies -

Ventures Resurgence, Keith Gleeson, 20, Madely Road, London, W.5.

Everly Brothers International, Ekerstraat 40b, Rotterdam 3021, Holland.

Elvis Presley, Maureen Fricker, 3, Orchard Villas, Old Perry Street, Chislehurst, Kent.

Bill Haley, Hugh McCallum, 26, Airedale Road, South Ealing, London, W.5.

Eddie Cochran, Mick Mirans, 50, Boundary Road, Ramsgate, Kent.

Jerry Lee Lewis, Wim de Boer, Dr. H.J.G. Hoebenstraat 12, Best, Holland. Malcolm Temple, 158, Ringland Circle, Newport, Mons.

Billy Fury, Tony Read, Court Bungalow, Frampton, Dorchester, Dorset.

Carl Perkins, Michael Cattin, Bois-Nois 41, 2300, La Chaux do Fonds, Switzerland.

Neil Sedaka, Mel Kirtley, 3, Hawkesly Road, Sunderland.

Little Richard, 26, Huntsman's Way, Rushey Mead, Leicester, LE4 7ZG.

MAIL ORDER RECORD LISTS

When you actually get around to buying R&R records, write off to all the mail order firms for samples of their lists. One of the most regular is 'Record Mart'. Really this is a magazine and not a list, but it differs from all other R&R magazines in that it has anything up to sixty pages of records for sale and auction. Costing 18½p, from 16, London Hill, Rayleigh, Essex, it is an essential publication as it keeps you up to date on current prices of records.

For size alone Hugh McCallum's auctions are a must; his lists consist of over eighty pages of foolscap listing anywhere up to 5,000 albums and singles. Many are very rare collectors' items but don't let that stop you bidding: there are usually some surprising bargains. When you write off for the lists, to the Bill Haley fan club address above, enclose a very, very large s.a.e.

For regularity of lists, Dan Reddington of 'Reddington's Rare Records, 20, Moor Street, Queensway, Birmingham B4, puts out six to ten sides of foolscap sheets that come through the mailbox with amazing punctuality. His singles retail around 50 to 75p each, and albums range from £1.50 to £2.50. You can pick up some very good sounds from Dan and he can be recommended.

Breathless Dan, not to be confused with Dan Reddington, also puts out some very educational lists, from his address at 'Rockhouse', 17, Graham Street, Bewport, Mons. His lists are excellent. Much of his stock is really rare.

In the London area there are one or two good places that issue lists. 'Moondogs', of 400, East Ham High Road North, London, E.12, have the best reputation; they've been going a long time as well. Their prices are very reasonable too. Just starting up in the mailing lists business is Pete Kickson of the 'Vintage Record Centre', 91, Roman Way, London, N.7. So far he has put out two massive lists listing all his stock over £1. This does not give any real indication of the stock in his shop, but more of that later.

Then there are the one-off people who suddenly decide to sell the whole of their collection, and here you must keep your eyes on the small ads column of 'Disc' and 'Sounds' magazines. These people are often the best of all as they often have no idea of the value of the records they are selling and tend to underprice them. Conversely, they often think they are worth more than they are and ridiculously overprice them.

ROCK AND ROLL RECORD SHOPS

Having received some of the above lists, it's time to go out into the wide world and get on with the searching. Be warned, however : record searching is a very hard habit to break once acquired. You may even find you are planning your holidays touring around the suburbs of darkest Manchester looking for little old shops with piles of dusty 78's. Again, be warned that there are thousands of other addicts with exactly the same thoughts as you and all the places named below are well used by them, but thankfully the proprietors seem able to replenish their stock almost immediately. You certainly won't find any 'only one ever pressed Elvis Presley Sun demonstration 78' for 50p, but you can guarantee coming away with some very useful additions to your collection.

London is the best place to start as it has more real R&R shops than any other city.

Vintage Record Centre, 91, Roman Way, London, N.7.

This shop is run by Pete Dickerson and Mike Gordon and is very near to the Caledonian Road Tube Station. Opening times are in the latter half of the week on Thursday afternoons and all day Saturday. Their stock is large and comprehensive coving R&R, Rockabilly, Pop, R&B, Blues,

Mersey etc., in fact every taste is catered for except jazz and classics. Prices start around 20p, and you can pick up some incredible bargains at very low prices. There are also 78's for sale.

Moondogs, 400, East Ham High Road North, London, E.12.

Run by Roger Ford this shop is about half a mile from East Ham Tube Station and is a goldmine for the serious collector of R&R, R&B and Soul. There are racks and racks of singles and albums, mainly imports all at various prices from around 25p each. Moondogs does not have a wide variety of styles of music, but tend to concentrate more on the U.S. R&R scene. They also sell magazines such as 'SMG' and 'Kommotion'.

Moxoms, 206, Forest Road, London, E.17.

This little-known shop is about 250 yards from Blackhorse Road Tube Station and it specialises in albums: there must be around 20,000 albums there. It has very few singles or E.P.'s though.

Whitechapel Market, London E.8.

Every Friday and Saturday directly outside Whitechapel Tube Station is a market stall. Singles start from just under 20p, albums are all sorts of prices.

Chris Wellard, Records, 6, Lewisham Way, London, S.E.14.

Run by John Gleckler this shop offers quite a few opportunities for you quickly and cheaply to extend your collection. Recently they had special offers on the Speciality label. The shop also has regular mail order lists of all types of music, mainly Rock and Blues.

Let It Rock, Kings Road, London, S.W.3.

Not just a record shop but one of those places where you can buy records, posters, drapes, string ties, shoes, the lot!!

Rock on, 93, Goldbourne Road, London, W.10.

This shop is on one of the roads that lead off the Portobello Road, and there are thousands of R&R and R&B singles here, often at very reasonable prices. There are a couple of other places in this and in Portobello Road worth visiting; they come and go, though, so just keep your eyes open.

Coventry Street, London, W.1.

Stuck in the back of one of those ghastly tourist souvenir shops is a fantastic little record stall run by John Dickens. He has a very large stock of mid-sixties singles on display, as well as some rarer records behind the counter. Also in stock is a large selection of Sun and Phillips singles, so Sun and Memphis addicts would have a field day here. Virtually next door in Coventry House on the third at Revival Records is Tony Martin. Tony is well into R&R and it would be well worth paying him a visit if you want to obtain any material from the 'Razorback' catalogue.

Roundabout, 7, North End Road, London, W.8/W.14.

If you collect mid-sixties or early sixties British R&R then this place is well worth a visit, and is the place to catch up on Marty Wilde/Cliff Richard/Billy Fury type records.

Record Exchange, 90, Goldhawk Road, London, W.12.

The ideal place for albums. A very good source of late fifties/early sixties albums as well as for recent compilations and re-issues.

Provincial Shops

Sound Unlimited, 149, North Street, Brighton, Sussex.

This is a fairly new shop, but the stock is getting larger.

Egleton & Chalmers, 26, Stanford Avenue, Hassocks, Sussex.

This shop has a superb selection of records which are also listed in the very comprehensive and regular lists. Recently they launched their 'Injun' record label and with half a dozen releases already under their belt it looks set to become a major label for R&R collectors.

Flyright Records, 47, Grange Road, New Haw, Weybridge, Surrey.

Flyright put out a regular rock list and distribute various obscure rock labels like Collector, Driving Wheel, and Splendid.

Shirley Road, Southampton.

Record Collectors' paradise here as there are actually two streets chock full of secondhand junk shops.

Browns, 146, Belgrave Gate, Leicester.

Could be worth looking in if your football team are playing in the second division. It used to have about 20,000 singles constantly on hand, but with ace collectors like Bob Fisher and Barry Lazell in the area I wouldn't hold out much hope of finding anything extra special.

Langleys, Bromley Hill, Downham, Bromley, Kent.

Langleys used to be the place to visit, but over the years its reputation has grown, and so the stock has decreased, sadly. Recently they were giving away their stock label by label for around 5 to 10p. It should still be worth visiting if you are in the area.

Bob Shop, Beau Belles Boutique, Rayners Lane, Pinner, Middlesex.

This has only a small stock of records, but like Langleys is worth the effort of visiting if you are in the area.

London Road, Croydon, Surrey.

There are at least two good shops in this area. The best one is at number 260 and virtually opposite a cinema. There are thousands and thousands of singles on show, but look behind the counter and you will see a few boxes : one marked R&R. Fifties singles start at about 65p. There are also hundreds of early sixties singles for 10p each.

Victoria Market, Southend, Essex.

There is one place here way up on the top floor and around the corner with thousands of singles and albums. As a matter of interest, if you buy a record, then the owner will give you a free ashtray!!

Simons Records, York Road, Southend, Essex.

There are a couple of racks here of R&R records and one of early soul and R&B. Southend is reputed to be one of the best centres in the whole of the UK for producing R&R fans, so Simons Records has a very fast turnover of stock.

Record Bar, 3, Tarring Road, Worthing, Sussex.

This shop has a very, very large stock of mid and late fifties' records including items by Gene Vincent, Bill Haley, Elvis, Buddy Holly, Sun 45's etc. They also put out mail order lists.

Kingston Market, Eden Street, Kingston-on-Thames, Surrey.

Two very long stalls here that will take you about an hour to sift through, and then there is a shop as well to look at behind the first stall. Certainly a must, as the stock is all fairly cheap.

Reddington's Rare Records, 20, Moor Street, Queensway, Birmingham 7.

The only place in the Midlands to concentrate on R&R, and what a place it is. There's enough here to keep you going for the whole of the afternoon. And if you need a break through looking at the records then start on the reading material plastered on the wall.

The above list consists of the best British shops worth visiting. Of course, as you start getting around to these places you will begin to find others that hold interesting stock. Eventually you will find that the real bargains come from tiny little junk shops situated in the most unlikely of places, or from the annual Oxfam High Street sale. There is a booklet available listing over three-hundred nationwide shops. It is called 'Shop Guide', and is available from 36, Scrapsgate Road, Minster, Sheppey, Kent, price 15p.

CREDITS

Special thanks to

Barry Lazell - who researched most of the biographies

Alice Lobb - who found many of the pictures and helped with the manuscript

And the dozens of friends, collectors, and record companies who helped make the discographies possible

Derek and Veronica Day - who provided a Little Richard pre-Speciality discography

Chris Savory - who researched the chapter 'How to collect Original 1950s Rock and Roll Records'.

Mike Leadbitter - who loaned the photos of Hank Ballard, The Coasters, Lloyd Price and Larry Williams

Pete Smart - who provided the biographical material on Jack Scott

Record Mirror and Melody Maker for the extensive use of their files

Pictures

Chalwest, Ltd. for the picture of the jukebox.

London Features International Ltd. for the picture of Fats Domino.

Barratt's Photo Press Ltd., for the picture of Duane Eddy The Camera Press and Rex Features.

London Express News and Features Service, for the Giles Cartoon.

'International Times', for 'Boppin'.

'Bye Bye Johnny', used by permission of Jewel Music Publishing Co. Ltd. (c) 1960 by Arc Music Corporation.

'Summertime Blues', used by permission of Cinephonic Music Co.

Printed by Flarepath Printers Limited, St. Albans, Herts.

Typesetting and art-work by Farringdon Press Limited, London, W. 14.